Exploring Nature

Written by Susie Alexander
Illustrations by Barb Lorseyedi
Cover by Cheri Macoubrie Wilson

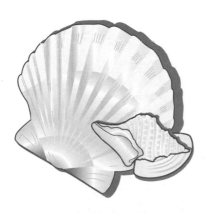

Teacher Created Materials

Teacher Created Materials, Inc.

6421 Industry Way

Westminster, CA 92683

© 1999 Teacher Created Materials, Inc.

Made in U.S.A.

www.teachercreated.com

ISBN #1-57690-362-1

Library of Congress Catalog Card Number: 96-061507

Editor:

Stephanie Buehler, M.P.W., M.A.

Table of Contents

Introduction

The world is an enormous place, from the tiniest insects to the largest trees, from the backyard to the farthest stars. The number of things to explore in nature is infinite. Children are natural-born scientists, constantly asking questions about the world they see. *Exploring Nature* will give you many ways to enjoy the beauty of nature with your young child.

As we introduce our children to all aspects of nature, we develop their curiosity, and we help take away their fear of the unknown. The younger the individual, the more you can help the child become familiar and comfortable with nature. You can also help your child develop a love for the outdoors in all its detail.

Nature gives you resources; *Exploring Nature* gives you ideas; and you provide opportunities. Your child's love for the world will flourish as a result. Get out your magnifying glass and collecting tools and enjoy the beauty of land, sky, and water through the eyes of a preschooler.

How to Use This Book

Exploring Nature is a manual for guiding young children through nature experiences. The book is easy to use. You can plan an outing around the places and activities suggested, or you can use the activities as follow-up to adventures that you and your child have already had. The book is divided into three sections: land, water, and sky. Within each of these sections are many topics divided into a number of fun-filled blocks that will give you things to think about and do with your child. Besides an introduction, you will find the following for each topic:

Walking Along . . .

There is no better way to understand nature than to visit a setting and experience it. This page at the beginning of each topic will give you specific ideas for nature walks.

Where to Go

These are suggested field trip activities for you and your child to take together. Some trips will suggest specific locations, such as a petting zoo, while others will suggest broad areas, like the desert.

What to Do

These are fun, post-experience activities, games, and crafts. Materials lists and easy-to-follow instructions will guide you through these simple projects. They are designed for your child to be able to do most of the work independently, but it will be all the more fun if you join in.

What Else?

This afterthought for each section includes either a novel piece of information or a piece of related literature.

Besides the activities in the land, water, and sky sections, *Exploring Nature* has many other uses. Because the best way to understand nature is to experience it, a section of this book is devoted to taking nature walks. "Going on a Nature Walk," beginning on page 8, will give you many new ideas for discovering nature in your own backyard or other places that your feet take you.

In "Extensions of Nature" (page 152), you will learn ways to document your child's explorations. Items included are nature journals and collection boxes. The bibliography and resources section lists nature-related fiction and non-fiction books, magazines, Web sites, and companies that might be of interest to you or your child. Each of these items will add to your time in nature. Although this book is a great resource for you and your family to enjoy during the preschool years, don't be surprised if you continue to use it for many years.

Safety Guidelines

If the primary goal in experiencing nature with your child is to enjoy it, the primary rule is to do so safely. If you observe a few rules of safety, you and your child will have a much better experience.

- Always stay with your child.
- Do not touch any plant animal or insect unless you can identify it and be sure it is safe. It is a good idea to carry a field manual to make identifications.
- Never touch a wild animal, alive or dead, no matter how cute it looks. It is vital that you warn your child against the dangers of touching wild animals—they can bite or carry diseases that can make humans very sick. No wild animal should ever be brought home as a pet.
- Always wear socks and shoes that cover the toes.
- In unfamiliar areas, you and your child should wear whistles. Instruct your child that if you get separated, he or she should stay in one place and blow the whistle until found.
- Check and follow posted rules in the areas you visit.
- Don't eat any plant items—especially mushrooms and berries.
- It's always a good idea to wash your hands at the end of an excursion.

Taking Longer Walks

Many nature walks will occur as you stroll about your neighborhood or other areas near your home. If you decide to take a nature walk farther than your normal walking area, your child may be more comfortable if you carry a few lightweight items in a backpack, such as the following:

- lightweight sweater
- water bottle
- healthy snack such as trail mix or crackers and cheese
- sunblock (reapply frequently)
- notebook with pencil
- flashlight, if walking after sundown
- wet wipes

Finally, for the safety and beauty of the plants, animals, and habitats you enjoy, remember to leave the environment as you found it.

6

Materials List

Here are some things you will want to keep around the house to be ready for a spontaneous adventure or craft related to nature.

Art Items

- tempera paints
- construction paper (especially black and blue)
- white drawing or copy paper
- colored markers
- permanent marker
- crayons
- paper plates
- string
- plaster of Paris
- coffee filters

Recycled Items

- cardboard egg cartons
- 2-liter soda bottles
- baby food jars

Items for Adult Use

The following items are needed for some of the projects in this book, but they are tools only an adult should use.

- fire/stove
- glass
- wooden skewers
- scissors
- craft knife

Going on a Nature Walk

Going on any kind of walk is an adventure for a preschooler. Strolling a mountain path, country orchard, or sandy beach, however, is a special experience. If your preschooler has experiences such as these, he or she is likely to grow up with fond and significant memories of nature. Here are some ways you can make walks in nature more purposeful and memorable, as well as a gentle teaching experience.

Hunt for a specific item. If you know that red-breasted robins or two-tailed swallowtails are dominant in your area, describe them to your child, and then search for them. Look in trees, on flowers and bushes, and in the air. Even if you don't find one, you will enjoy the journey.

Look for patterns in nature. Look for shapes in or on objects; you may be surprised how many shapes you and your child can find, such as those made by branches crossed in a tree. Pattern walks also work well. A pebble thrown into a stream makes concentric circles, while ants march in an orderly line. You will enjoy pointing out the world's unique beauty, while your child will be in wonder at how the world is arranged.

Do a color search. Try looking for red items in nature, for example. Visual exploration games like this are good for introducing critical thinking skills to your preschooler.

Make up your own pattern. Find one squirrel, two blue jays, three pansies, four elm trees, etc. As a variation, look for just five of an item, or let your child decide how many of each object you will find together.

Collect treasures. Remember when you were five and a crimson leaf or a pigeon feather was as exciting as a trip to the zoo? In our high-tech society, we sometimes forget that nature is its own reward for children. Help your child discover some treasures on your walk, and it won't be long before he or she is adding to the collection. (See page 152 for ideas on storing nature collections.)

8

Going on a Nature Walk (cont.)

Take a Quiet Walk. Enjoy a walk with your child with a single rule—no talking, but pointing and smiling are definitely allowed. If your child is interested, upon returning from your walk, make a list of all of the sounds you heard.

Noises in Nature. Your preschooler will be happy to demonstrate how to take a noisy walk. How many ways can your child make noise without using his or her voice? How about crunching leaves? splashing in puddles? tapping on trees, the ground, and bushes with a stick? Making noises in nature is fun.

Have a Recycling Race. To have a productive walk, take along a couple of plastic bags and collect trash along the way. Use the plastic bag or wear gloves to pick up trash. The winner (who will, of course, be your child) will be the one with the fullest bag. Also, it is thoughtful to leave nature more beautiful than you first saw it.

All of these walking games will be entertaining to a preschooler, but the most important part for the child will be just getting out and about with someone who loves him or her. Nature doesn't need gimmicks, and your time together can be special because it is just the two of you in the big, beautiful world. Don't worry if he or she doesn't want to play your way—take your cues from your little one and enjoy the serenity of nature.

Land

Walking to See Plants

The most dominant things your child will notice on a nature walk will be hundreds of species of plants, trees, and flowers. Plants cover so much of our world that we often take them for granted. With just a little encouragement, however, a young child will count trees or point out the different types of plants and flowers as she skips along. During any walk, you will find many plants to see, smell, and even gently touch.

If you are walking in an area that is especially lush, this is a perfect time for a quiet walk in which you use the senses of sight, sound and smell. Practice zipping your lips before you head off and join in the quiet fun, speaking only to give reminders on issues of safety.

To make the walk a learning experience, point out that different plants grow in different areas called habitats. You won't find a cactus in the jungle, and you won't find an elm tree in the desert. Each plant has its own very special home where it can grow best.

A magnifying glass can be a useful tool to inspect the more intricate details of leaves, flowers, seeds, and bark. Take along a tape measure, too. Show your child how you can measure leaves and then have a contest to see who can find the largest, smallest, widest, and narrowest leaves.

As you enjoy plants through the eyes of your child, you will be seeing a whole world you may have forgotten. Allow yourself to be awed by tiny seeds and monstrous oaks.

One caution—be on the lookout for these "itchy" plants!

 #2362 Exploring Nature

Seed Deeds

Studying seeds with preschoolers is fascinating—how can an entire apple tree grow from a seed smaller than a fingernail? Many young children know where seeds come from, but the cycle of seed-to-plant-to-fruit-to-seed eludes them. Be sure to explain this cycle as you eat fruit or find a seed pod during a walk.

The seed actually contains almost all of the parts it needs to become the plant it is supposed to be; it only requires sunlight, earth, and water to help it along. Prove this to your child by soaking a bean for a couple of hours, and then pulling it open with your fingernail. What you will see are the beginnings of a little plant. Some fun questions to ask include the following:

- How do you think a tiny seed becomes a big tree?
- Why do fruits and vegetables have so many seeds inside of them?
- What do you think is the biggest seed? (The answer to this one is on page 16, in case you yourself don't know.)

Where to Go

The natural time to discover and investigate seeds is during the spring and autumn months. Spring is when most seeds sprout. Anywhere you walk in nature, you will find seeds or things that come from seeds. Ask your child, How do you think this plant got here? What do you think is under the ground?

During the autumn months, you will find empty pods from trees that will be fun to look at through a magnifying glass. In fact, because seeds are so small, a magnifying glass is a piece of science equipment that should be used with every seed activity.

At nurseries, study flower seed packets with your child. Explain that you can't just buy seeds because the plant pictured on the package is pretty. You have to consider the environment for each flower and plant. Some need lots of sun, while others need very little. Explain that growing flowers and plants can be very complicated because each one needs just the right type of earth and the right amount of sun and water to grow.

What to Do

Grow Your Own Seedlings

To prove seeds contain plants, you can do this magical experiment.

Materials

- clear plastic cup
- beans
- paper towels
- water

Directions

Fold a few paper towels and put them around the inside of the cup. Stuff a balled paper towel into the center. Place a couple of large beans around the sides between the paper towels and the cup. (For best results, soak the beans for a couple of hours prior to putting them in the cup.) Dampen the paper towels, and keep them damp over the next week or so while the seeds begin to sprout. When the seedlings begin to form leaves, pull the seedlings out and plant them in your garden.

Play Seed Packet Concentration

This is a new twist on the old game of concentration that your child will quickly learn to play. Show your child pairs of flower, fruit, and vegetable seed packets. Mix them up and lay them upside down on the floor. Your child will pick them up two at a time until he or she has a match. Play until all packets have been matched. (Remind your gardening friends to save their empty packets for you.)

What Else?

Read the book *The Carrot Seed* by Ruth Krauss. Children love this simple book, especially when the young main character is right and no one else thinks he will be.

Create Egg Faces With Grassy Hair

This great seed craft is guaranteed to work.

Materials

- egg shells
- bleach
- permanent markers
- soil
- grass seed
- water

Directions

After you have used a cleanly cracked egg, wash the shell with soap, water, and bleach. After it is thoroughly dry, use a permanent marker to put a face on the shell, with the egg opening at the top of the head. Fill the egg with soil or peat moss and sprinkle a teaspoon of seeds on top. Spray with water; keep the soil damp. Store the filled egg in a leftover egg carton. Very soon the seeds will sprout, giving the egg face a green head of hair. Trim as desired.

What Else?

Guess how many seeds will be inside a piece of fruit before you cut it open.

Sorting Beans

Sorting is an important preschool activity that, besides being a lot of fun, teaches visual discrimination. Purchase a bag of assorted beans from the grocery store. Start with packages containing only three or four types of beans and progress to the more varied collections as your child becomes good at sorting. Pour a cup full of beans into a plastic bowl, and show your child how to sort the beans by their visual characteristics into separate muffin tins. Place, for example, all of the red beans in one cup, all of the large white ones in another cup, etc. This is a good activity to keep children occupied while you are preparing dinner. Be sure your child knows not to put the beans in his nose or mouth. Also, be sure toddlers can't reach for the beans.

Guess the Seed

As your child becomes more experienced with seeds, he will soon be able to identify them, especially if you introduce this game. Using seed packets, choose two seeds out of each one. Keep one in a bowl and tape the other to the back of the packet. Have the child match the seeds to the picture on the seed packets. He can do a self-check by looking at the backs of the packets when he is finished.

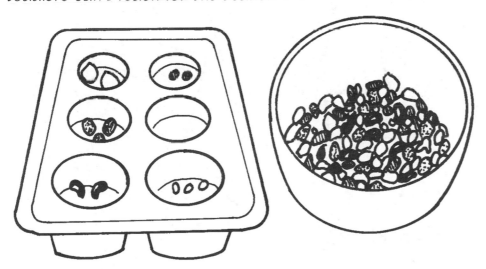

Seed Mosaics

Here's a pretty art project that preschoolers love.

Materials

- lightweight cardboard
- pen
- white glue
- cotton swab
- variety of beans

Directions

Mosaics can be very intricate and detailed. However, when making seed mosaics with preschoolers, use a large, simple pattern. On the cardboard, draw some simple shapes, such as a circle within a larger circle placed within a triangle. Pour some glue in the middle of the cardboard. Show your child how to use a cotton swab to smear it around. Make sure your child understands that the seeds will stick only where there is glue.

Use materials with strong contrast for the most texture, like sesame seeds, kidney beans, black-eyed beans, and dried peas.

What Else?

What is the largest seed? The coconut! Have your child guess what is inside one, and then cut it open.

Pretty Plants

Plants are important to our world. The green leaves make food for themselves using sunlight and water. During this process, called photosynthesis, leaves release oxygen into the air. This is great for humans because we need the oxygen to breathe. Plants are also important because they form the basis of the food chain, providing nourishment for insects, animals, and people. We couldn't live if there weren't any plants around!

This section focuses on plants that do not produce flowers or fruit. You can ask your child questions that will get her mind thinking about plant life. for example, Why are there so many different kinds of plants? Why do leaves on plants come in so many shapes and sizes?

Where to Go

Any park, large or small, is a great place to observe, enjoy, and compare different types of plants.

Your neighborhood nursery will also contain a variety of green plants. Show your preschooler the tag in each pot that identifies the plant by a familiar name and a scientific name. Hearing the scientific names may give her a giggle because it will sound so different from everyday language. Explain that plants have two names, a common one and a scientific one written in Latin.

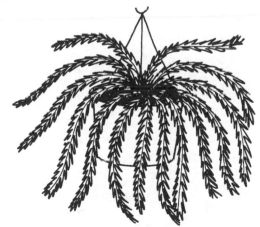

Besides the beautiful and exotic flowers for which they are known, arboretums usually have greenhouses for unique varieties of plants. Find out if you are permitted to gently touch the vegetation. Have your child feel the different textures of leaves: smooth, bumpy, fuzzy, etc.

What to Do

Growth Conditions Experiment

What do plants need in order to grow? Don't just tell your child; show her!

Materials

- three identical seedlings from a nursery, hardware, or discount store.

Directions

Keep one seedling outside where it will receive a few hours of daily sun. Put one in your house on a table where it will receive some indirect sunlight. Place the last seedling in a closet. Give all the plants the same amount of water. What does your child think will happen? How long will it take before you see a definite difference?

Demonstrate the Parts of Plants

Looking at what is under the soil is sometimes just as exciting as looking at what is above it! With a trowel, dig up a large weed or unwanted plant. Brush and wash off any excess dirt to get a good look at the roots. Ask why plants have these special parts. Then explain that as the plant grows up, it also grows down to get water and nutrients from the soil.

What Else?

Most plants enjoy sunshine and water as a stable diet, but there are some varieties of plants that are actually meat-eaters. These sticky, tricky plants lure insects and digest them. Sometimes you can find these novelty plants, such as Venus fly traps, at children's science centers or specialty nurseries. If not, ask the children's librarian for a book that has pictures of these unusual plants.

18

Make a Terrarium

Materials

- empty, clean mayonnaise jar with lid
- small pebbles or gravel
- sand
- soil
- small plants or cuttings like ferns, rhododendron, and moss
- straw or spoon
- small plastic animals (optional)

Directions

Layer a few of inches of gravel, followed by a few inches of sand in the jar. Shake it back and forth to make an even mixture. Gently add soil. Sprinkle some water in the jar, and then use a straw or spoon to stir the soil and make it thoroughly moist. Push the small plants into the soil with the straw. Add plastic animals to create a fictional

setting. When you are pleased with how the terrarium looks, cap the jar and watch this little habitat take care of itself.

Make Mushroom Art

Use a mushroom to make a special pattern.

Materials

- ripe, store-bought mushrooms of various sizes
- white paper
- plastic containers, like yogurt or sour cream containers

Directions

Break the stalks off the mushrooms. Place the mushroom caps flat on the paper and cover them with the plastic containers. Leave them alone for about three hours. When you return, gently remove the plastic containers and lift off the mushrooms. What is left? The spores from the mushrooms have fallen to produce one of nature's patterns.

For other related activities, see sections on leaves, seeds, and trees.

Match Plants with Their Habitats

Every habitat supports different forms of life. Can your child guess which plants grow where? On the left side of the page are a number of plants that grow especially well in particular habitats. On the right are those habitats. Help your child understand why certain things grow better in some conditions than others. (Answers are on page 160.)

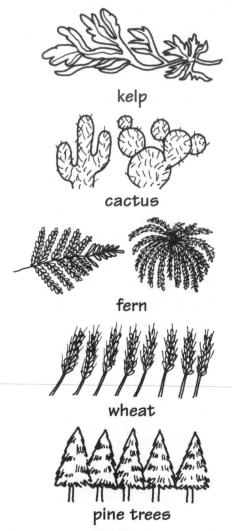

kelp

cactus

fern

wheat

pine trees

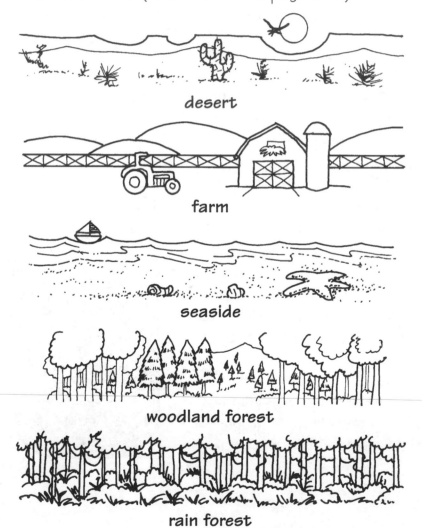

desert

farm

seaside

woodland forest

rain forest

20

Flower Fun

Spring and summer are seasons filled with flowers, though you will see some varieties bloom even during fall and winter. Small children aren't the only ones who enjoy the many scents and colors of these creations. As you walk along, don't forget that flowers are a perfect tie-in for color identification and reinforcement.

As you have probably noticed, different flowers grow in different conditions: some in shade, some in direct sunlight, some in wet soil, some in dry.

This is beneficial, as flowers are food for animals in different types of homes. Some flowering plants and trees later produce fruit. The fruit grows from the blossoms.

Look at the illustration of a flower and its parts. Of course, not every flower will be the same as this one because each type of flower is different. This picture will give you a general idea of the parts of flowers are called.

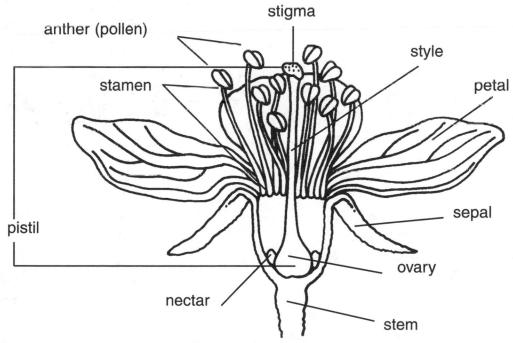

Where to Go

Visit a nursery in your area during the spring and early summer for a detailed look at seeds, budding plants, and many different types of flowers. Ask your child such questions as, "Why do you think there are so many different colors? Do you think the birds and bees like some flowers better than others? Which flower would you like to be if you could choose? Which one smells the nicest and most fragrant?"

Flower shops are a perfect place to enjoy flowers all year long. If you are able, buy a bunch of flowers to take home and examine. Compare the flower parts to those in the illustration on page 21. How are they the same? How are they different?

Go on a flower color scavenger hunt. On a piece of paper, make a column of colored squares. (Red, orange, yellow, purple would be good choices.) Next to the squares, put a line or a box. Have your child identify flowers of those colors—he or she can draw pictures of them next to the colored squares or you can write in the name of the flower.

Arboretums are homes to special selections of rare flowers and plants. Often you will find exotic, rain forest vegetation. This may be the most close-up view of these special flowers that you or your little one will ever see, making it well worth the excursion.

What to Do

Make 3-D Rainbows

From the flowers grown in your own garden, you can create a special rainbow that has texture as well as color.

Materials

- two paper plates
- white glue
- small plastic bags
- scissors
- cotton swabs
- various flower petals

Directions

Cut out a rainbow shape from half a paper plate. Pencil in curved lines. Go on a hunt for petals from three or four different-colored flowers, collecting them in plastic bags to take home. (Ask permission from neighbors before taking any flower petals.) Put the various petals in piles on a paper plate. Pour some glue into one rainbow section and spread with a cotton swab. Press all the petals of

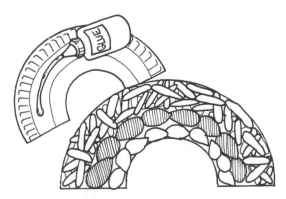

one color into the section. Do the same with each section, using a different color each time. Be sure to take a picture of the end product because, though pretty, it will not last long.

What Else?

Flowers are often used in decorating. How many places can your child find flowers around your house? Look at upholstery, dishes, pillows, and wallpaper. You can do this activity when you visit the housewares department of any store, too. Explain the difference between real flowers and imitations that look quite real

Make a Daisy Chain

Every child has to make a daisy chain necklace at least once. With a fingernail or paring knife (only to be used by an adult), make a short slit, about 1/2" (1.3 cm), in the stem near the flower. Slide a second daisy into the slit. Make the next slit below where the flower went into the first one. Continue with all flowers. When working with a child, prepare a bunch of flowers with slits and let the child experiment with putting them together. Chains are also fun to make with clovers and rose buds.

What Else?

Read a tale that describes beautiful flowers, *Miss Rumphius* by Barbara Cooney. You will feel as if you were lost in a field of wildflowers while reading this enchanting book.

Flower Magic

This is a vivid and colorful demonstration of how water and nutrients travel to feed the flower part of the plant.

Materials

- white carnation
- two small cups of water
- two colors of food coloring
- scissors

Directions

Add a few drops of food coloring to each of the cups of water. Carefully slit the stem of the carnation almost to the flower. Place half of the stem in one cup and half in the other cup. Come back in a couple of hours and you will see a changed flower.

Make a Vase

Make a wild vase for some wild flowers. Cut off the neck and upper portion of a clean, plastic drinking-water bottle. On the bottle, draw designs or patterns in colored permanent markers. (Water-based markers will not adhere to the plastic bottle. Let your child color the bottle outside while wearing an old shirt if you are concerned about stains.) Tie a raffia bow around the bottle and fill with flowers and water.

What Else?

Read Lois Ehlert's book, *Plant a Rainbow*. This terrific book uses color words to talk about many varieties of flowers.

Dry Some Flowers

Find your favorite flowers and make them last forever. Flowers that are not flat dry better than those that are; roses are a perfect choice for drying. Attach a thin corkboard strip under a kitchen cabinet. Trim the flower stem so that all leaves, thorns, etc., are removed. Turn the flower upside down and attach the end of the stem to the corkboard. Within a few days, the moisture from the flower will have dried out.

What Else?

An especially fun flower is the snapdragon. If you pinch the sides, it will open its snapping "mouth," a complete delight to any child.

Have a Garden Tea Party

With all the imagination preschoolers have, this will be the best tea party ever. You can use "leftover" items in your garden for the makings of an adorable tea party. Start with acorn hulls to make perfect little cups. Pansies and impatiens (or any flat flower) can become plates. Seeds and pods are the food. Serve these delicate items on a large, flat leaf as a place mat. Make it clear that these items are for pretend; none of them are safe to eat.

Eat a Flower

Here is a floral tea party that really is edible. Make this salad and see how adventurous your preschooler can be.

- spinach or romaine lettuce
- nasturtiums
- tomato
- oil & vinegar dressing

Wash all vegetables and flowers thoroughly. Tear lettuce into bite-sized pieces, chop tomato, and pull blossoms off of nasturtium stems. Toss with dressing and serve. (Be sure to tell your child that most flowers are inedible and never to be eaten.)

For related activities, see the sections on seeds, plants, and trees.

26

Life With Trees

Trees are fascinating to children because they are huge.

You can identify trees by their leaves, bark, and seeds. There are two major classifications of trees: deciduous (flat leaf) or hardwood trees and conifer (evergreen) or softwood trees. Animals and people use trees as an important source of food and housing. Fruit that grows on the branches, crunchy green leaves, seeds and cones that fall to the ground, and the insects burrowed in the bark are the diet of many wild animals. We use the wood to make our houses, but animals and insects actually live in, on, or under trees, even using them as camouflage to keep themselves safe from predators.

Besides their many uses, there is nothing quite as relaxing as sitting under the shade of a big tree with a good book to read. Try this activity with your little one today.

Where to Go

Most parks have many different types of trees. Take along a field book with lots of great pictures and compare the trees in the book to the ones you find at the park. Which ones have flowers? fruit? leaves that change color? needles?

Compare large and small trees. Find some seeds or pods and explain how every tree has started from a single seed. Trees are all so different!

Our country's national parks contain some very old trees. Because they are protected by law, they are a national treasure we'll be able to hand down to our children and grandchildren. Visit a national park and have your child notice the different types of leaves on trees. If you are walking in an area sheltered with trees, notice how long you can stay in their shade. If you are interested in finding a nearby national park, check the Internet sources in the Resources section of this book (page 157).

Private and commercial nurseries have a great variety of trees. They won't mind if you wander around admiring their selection, but be extremely gentle when examining bark and leaves.

Walking through an orchard makes a wonderful excursion. The unique thing about an orchard is that all of the trees look virtually the same. Close your eyes and see if you can tell what type of fruit grows in the orchard by the scent that surrounds you.

What to Do

Make a Bark Rubbing

Nature is full of texture, and it is fun to actually see the texture come alive in a rubbing.

Materials

- white copy or tracing paper
- crayons with paper wrappers removed

Directions

Take your paper and crayons along on your walk. Hold the paper onto the trunk of a tree and have your child do the rubbing with the wide part of the crayon. It looks especially nice to have rows of rubbings from four or five different trees done with different colors on the same paper.

Discover the Age of a Tree

Every tree holds a mystery—its age. When a tree on your property needs removal, get out your saw and discover the answer to a tree's age. Saw a clean line through a tree trunk and notice the rings. As the tree grows each year, it adds a ring. Estimate how many years you think the tree has been around, and then count the rings from the inside out to find the age of the tree. If you cannot do this activity, go to the library and find a book with an illustration of tree rings.

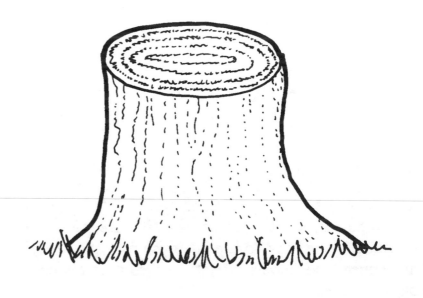

Paint Trees for the Seasons

Seeing trees during the four seasons is a perfect way to develop an appreciation of change in nature.

Materials

- brown tempera paint
- brush
- butcher paper
- colored markers

Directions

On a piece of butcher paper, you are going to make four trees standing next to one another, using your child's arm and hand as the brush. Each of the trees will represent a season. Paint the inside of your child's arm (trunk) and hand (branches) with the brown paint. Press the hand and arm onto the butcher paper four times. (Paint will need to be reapplied.) After the trees dry, decorate each with colored markers according to the season: spring with green leaves, summer with pink blossoms, fall with colored leaves (some can be drifting down out of the tree and on the ground), and winter with a bare tree.

What Else?

Most people identify trees by overall stature and the shape of their leaves. But did you know that another good way to distinguish one tree from another is by the bark? Be sure to employ your child's sense of touch by exploring the trees with your hands.

Janice Udry's Caldecott Award-winning book, *A Tree Is Nice*, is a perfect complement to a day spent among trees.

Sticks Pencil Holder

Make a fun gift with something you can find easily during your nature walks.

Materials

- frozen orange juice can, cleaned with bleach
- spray paint
- sticks
- white glue
- colored ribbon

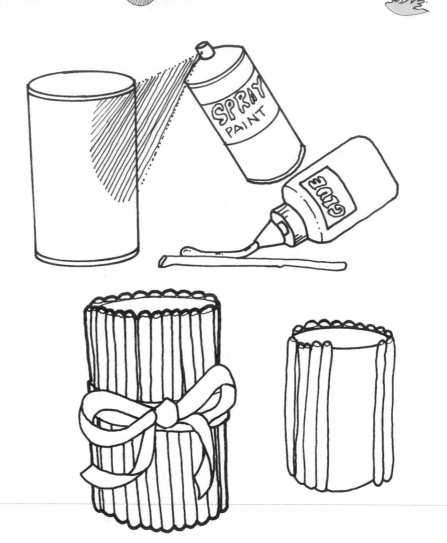

Directions

Collect similarly-sized sticks from the ground as you take a walk. Spray paint the can a solid color of your choice as a base. Break the sticks into pieces that are long enough to cover most of the can. Put some glue on each stick and adhere it to the outside of the can. Continue gluing sticks around the can until it is covered. When the glue has dried, tie a pretty ribbon around the can.

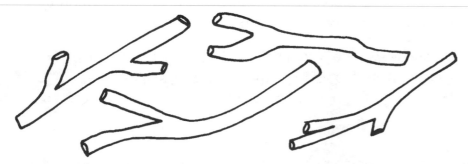

What Else?

Ask your child to guess the name of the biggest tree. The largest tree that is currently alive is a giant sequoia, standing at 365 feet (110 m)—one quarter the size of the Empire State Building.

Plant a Tree

There is nothing like the experience of digging a big hole and planting your own tree. This is the perfect time to explain about tree roots and why trees need them for nourishment and growth. Before you put your contribution to nature in the ground, be sure your child has a chance to feel the roots and talk about their function. You can also discuss the types of trees that grow well in your area and the conditions they need.

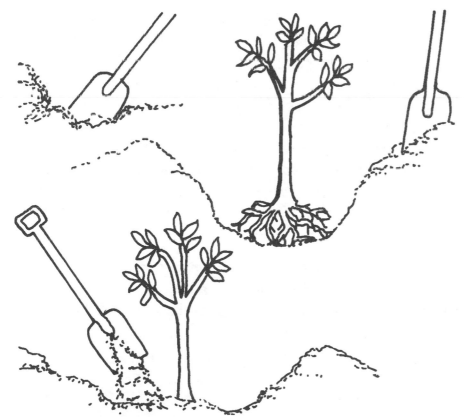

Go on a Tree Hunt in Your Own Home

We use trees for many things. How many ways can your little one find that trees have been used around your house? Set the timer for three minutes. Walk around the house and yard with your child and see how many things are made out of wood. He will probably notice large pieces of furniture, but don't let him forget door frames and doors, picture frames, and hardwood floors. If your child is ready for the concept, explain that paper is made from trees that have been ground up and mixed with water and other chemicals. Now how many things can he find that are made from trees? For other related activities, see the sections on leaves, plants, and seeds.

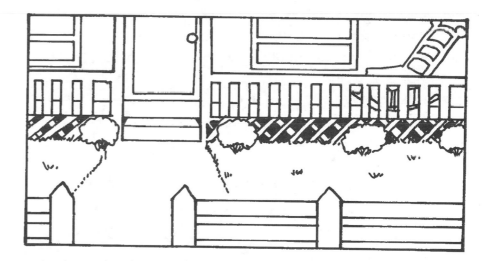

What Else?

Read about some of the many purposes of trees in Dick Gackenbach's book, *Mighty Tree*.

All Kinds of Leaves

Leaves are wonderful to investigate because of their variety. Some are large, some are small; some are flat, some have big veins; some are pointy, some are rounded. And then there are the colors! Leaves are important to plants because they absorb sunlight. That is part of the process of photosynthesis, which is the way plants manufacture their own food.

Show your child the parts of some leaves through a magnifying glass. The veins act as strong ribs holding the leaf together and keeping it firm. Point out to her the veins in her wrists or arms and explain how they take nutrients in blood around the body, just like these veins take nutrition to the rest of the leaf.

APEX

VEIN

MIBRIB

BONE

STEM

Ask your child some questions about leaves, such as, Why do you think the leaves change color? Why are some leaves pointed and others rounded? What is your favorite color on a leaf?

Where to Go

It is part of the amazing nature of the plant world that all plants have many of the same characteristics: seed, stem, leaves, blossoms. Anywhere you go for a walk, your child will be able to point leaves out to you. So when you take a leaf walk, make it special. Look for certain colors, shapes, and sizes. Look for the tree with the least amount of leaves or none at all. Compare the difference between healthy leaves and dying ones. Ask your child why some leaves are so pretty and green and others are shriveled and brown. Forests, backyards, neighborhoods, orchards—anywhere there are plants is a great place to enjoy leaves.

You can also manufacture your own nature walk, visiting a florist or searching for leaves at a nursery or florist shop. This is a great way for an errand to become a field trip.

What to Do

Leaf Rubbings

This classic children's favorite is a magical experience for young children.

Materials

- white copy or tracing paper
- crayons with paper wrappers removed
- leaves

Directions

Place a leaf, vein side up, on a table. Put a piece of white paper over it. Show your child how to use the side of a crayon to rub back and forth over the leaf area. Use a variety of colors and leaves for a pretty leaf-rubbing collage.

Leaf Tallies

Take along a piece of paper and pencil on your walk and make a tally mark for each plant or tree that has leaves of a certain type. For instance, you may want to focus on leaf color. On your paper, make columns for red, yellow, brown, green, and mixed. As you notice the leaves, have your child decide which category the leaves fall into and make a tally mark in that column. (Be sure to show how to make the fifth mark go across the others to make counting by fives easy.) For very young children, make a few outlines of leaves and color them in as you find trees of various colors.

What Else?

Read *Say It!* by Charlotte Zolotow is fun to read after a good run in the fall leaves.

Leaf Prints

Your child may very well laugh as you demonstrate this activity in which you beat a leaf to make a print, but she will be surprised by the colorful result.

Materials

- leaves
- two pieces of white paper or light fabric
- tape
- hammer or rock

Directions

Find a couple of brightly colored green leaves. Lay them between two pieces of paper or white, light fabric and tape the paper down in a couple of places. With a rock or hammer, pound onto the top piece over the area where leaves lay underneath. When you are done pounding, you will have a pretty, green, leaf design.

What Else?

If you have been outside on a windy fall day, your child will enjoy imitating the falling leaves, especially if you play the part of the wind and blow on him or her.

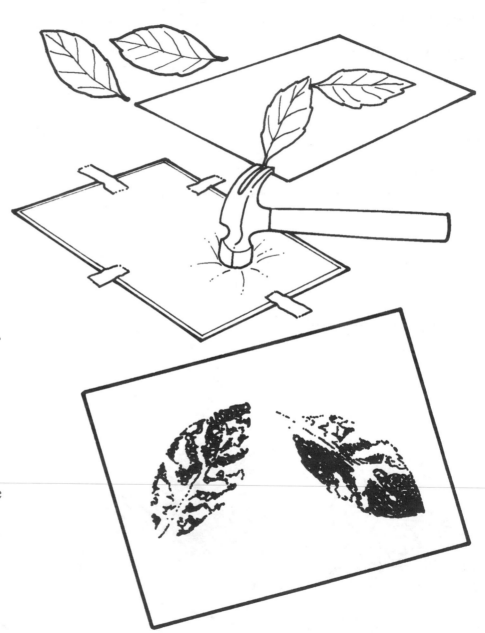

Eat All Your Fruits and Vegetables

Fruits and vegetables allow adults and children to experience nature with all of the senses. Because children are so used to seeing these items as food, it may be hard for them to relate to them as part of nature. Expand your child's perspective by helping him or her to see that every fruit and vegetable is a product from a plant or tree.

Fruits and vegetables grow in many different ways. Some, like apples and peaches, come from trees. Pumpkins, grapes, and some berries are examples of products grown from vines. Pineapples grow as a fruit on a bush, and the potato grows underground as a tuber. Ask your child what type of tree a carrot or potato grows on to see if she knows about vegetables that grow in the soil. Because they are filled with vitamins, vegetables and fruits pulled right off the tree, vine, or plant are healthy food for anyone to enjoy. (Remember to wash them first, though.)

Where to Go

Visit a farm or orchard. There are many farms that welcome visitors, especially those that grow seasonal items like apples or pumpkins. When you are in an orchard or on a farm, you can have a good look at the difference between good and bad fruit.

Don't forget the produce section of the grocery store or fruit market. It may not seem like nature, but everything there came from the outdoors. If your child is learning the alphabet, see if the two of you can name fruits and vegetables that begin with the letters of the alphabet: A for apple, B for banana, etc.

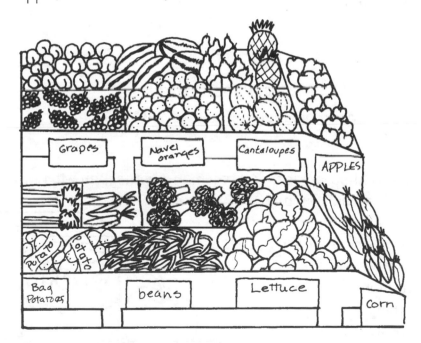

A country fair will show your child the rewards of the farmer's labor. It will give you more opportunities to talk about where fruits and veggies come from and how important farmers are to us.

What to Do

Homemade Applesauce

It is important for preschoolers to see the process of how products are made, so try this easy recipe. The best part for young children to do is the stirring, but take special care around the stove.

Ingredients

- 1 lb. apples (Macintosh are best)
- water to cover
- sugar to taste (you won't need much)
- 1 t. cinnamon, more or less to taste

Directions

Peel and chop apples. Put them in a saucepan with water just to cover. Simmer for about an hour, stirring occasionally. Add sugar and cinnamon and cook a few minutes more. Serve warm (not hot!), at room temperature, or refrigerated. Homemade applesauce is yummy over ice cream, too!

What Else?

Name all the things you can do with an apple.

Read *Rain Makes Applesauce* by J. Schew. It won't take long for your child to be reading the repetitive phrases in this book along with you.

Fruit and Vegetable Stamping

This is a favorite preschooler activity.

Materials

- primary color tempera paints
- pie pan for each paint color
- paper
- clear shelf paper (optional)
- assorted fruits & vegetables:
  — one citrus fruit
  — two apples, one cut horizontally and one vertically
  — carrot
  — mushroom
  — broccoli, cut down the middle
  — half a potato

Directions

Dip each fruit or veggie in paint and stamp it onto the paper. Show the child that he or she does not have to press hard onto the paper to make a print and that multiple prints can be made each time the stamper is dipped in paint. Fruit prints make beautiful designs. Turn the prints into placemats by covering them with clear shelf paper. You can also have them professionally laminated at a copy store.

What Else?

Recite this cute rhyme that will also help your child with ordering the months of the year:

Apples, peaches, pears, and plums,
Tell me when your birthday comes:
January, February, March . . .
(Jump up when your birthday month is spoken.)

Fruit Kabobs

Having fruit for lunch will never be the same once you have let your preschooler prepare it this way.

Ingredients

Cut the following fruits into wedges, sections, or chunks:

- cantaloupe
- apples
- watermelon
- pineapple (a can of chunk pineapple is fine)
- grapes

Directions

Soak some wooden skewers, and show your child how to make a pattern with the pieces of fruit on the skewer. Rub some of the pineapple chunks over the apple pieces to keep them from turning brown.

Fruit and Veggie Riddles

You can make up these riddles anytime, giving hints about the characteristics of your chosen food. Here are a couple of examples:

> I'm something small and green that comes in bunches and grows on a vine. What am I?

> I'm yellow; you don't eat the outside of me; I'm a monkey's favorite food. What am I?

Your child will love making these up as much as he or she enjoys answering them.

What Else?

A wonderful fruit and vegetable book is Lois Ehlert's *Eating the Alphabet*. Before you open the book, can you think of any produce that begins with X or Z?

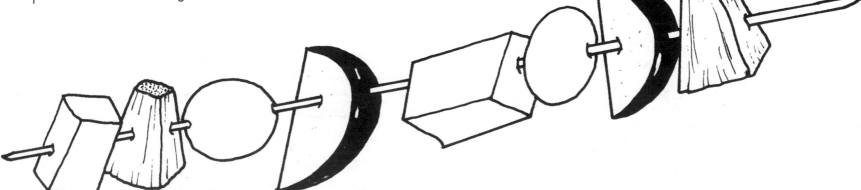

38

Grow Carrot Tops

Here is one of the easiest ways to demonstrate plant growth.

Materials

- carrot top with greens removed
- shallow dish
- water

Directions

Put the carrot top in the shallow dish, and add just enough water to cover the carrot, but not to its very top. Over the next few days continue adding water as it evaporates. Soon green sprouts will appear on the top of the carrot again, just like the original carrot. Because we often buy carrots with the greens already removed or in a bag, your child may be surprised to see something growing. Make sure he has a chance to see carrots with greens in the produce department, and point out that carrots grow in the ground, while the greens grow above the earth.

Make Roots

This old standby activity is fun for showing the part of a plant we usually can't see, the roots.

Materials

- sweet potato
- toothpicks
- glass of water

Directions

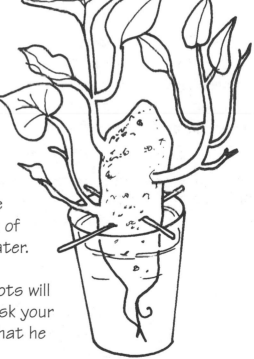

Insert at least four toothpicks around the center of the circumference of the sweet potato. Place the sweet potato into the glass so that the toothpicks rest along the edges. Cover the bottom of the sweet potato with water. As the water begins to evaporate, add more. Roots will soon start to develop. Ask your child what he sees and what he thinks roots are for.

Gardening with Preschoolers

Planting seeds is a wonder to a young child. It doesn't take much space or even patience to grow a garden. Introduce this activity to your child as soon as possible and the memories will also begin to grow.

Start simple and small. You will want to select seeds that sprout quickly, such as marigolds, tomatoes, zucchini, beans, and herbs. Mark off an area of the garden for your child to work in and have as her own. Give simple instructions and let her do the work. Then, when she reaps the rewards, they will be hers alone to cherish. Child-size gardening tools are available through educational toy stores, nature stores, and children's supply catalogs (see page 157).

Making things simple is the key, so plant your seeds directly into a cardboard egg carton, putting a few seeds in each egg cup. Then pour in some dirt with a spoon and sprinkle with water, using either a children's watering can or a sprayer. Once the seedlings start to sprout, pull out the less sturdy ones. (Be sure to follow the instructions on the seed packet for more specific planting instructions.) In the section of land you have set aside for your little one, dig a hole that the egg carton will fit into. Gently place the carton into the dirt, and pat the dirt around it. Eventually, the carton will disintegrate, leaving healthy, happy plants!

Then the real fun starts. Show your child the difference between a weed and a seedling. Many a baby plant has been pulled due to lack of information. Your child will enjoy daily weeding and watering as she watches her plants grow and develop. This would be a great activity to be recorded in a picture or nature journal, as your child sees the process of life in plants.

Once your child has experience with growing simple-to-start plants, you might want to expand your garden to attract some interesting new creatures. Trumpet vines and hibiscus flowers attract hummingbirds, for example. Watch hummingbirds in your area to see what other types of flowers they enjoy. Plants that attract butterflies include hyssop, sage, lantana, and lavender—depending on the type of butterfly you would like to see. Check a nature store for books and information on attracting these and other interesting creatures to your yard.

Walking with Animals

There is a special relationship between children and animals, but taking nature walks to appreciate animals will require some special skills on the part of your preschooler. The commands to be gentle, quiet, or still will have new meaning for your child when they're used on a nature walk during which animals make their appearance. As parents, we want our children to obey, but often they don't understand our urgency. When you point out a squirrel next to a tree or a rabbit scampering across a field, your child will quickly see the consequences of his actions if he doesn't stand still and be quiet. The lessons nature teaches are sometimes quite subtle.

The most important safety rule in appreciating animals on nature walks is not to touch them. Some of them may be frightened, some may respond with aggression. Animals carry dangerous diseases, too, that are harmful to humans. Be safe and always encourage your child to look instead of touch.

Walks are a good time to point out that any place you step is the potential home to some animal It is important not to disturb their habitats or leave trash behind.

Animals can teach us so many lessons about hard work, being prepared, caring for a family, and the importance of play. Help your child understand the world of animals by spending some time together with an animal.

Animal Games

Try these simple educational games with your preschooler to see what he or she knows about animals. Because most preschoolers cannot read, use the games as an oral language activity. These games are great to use in the car or while walking. As you learn more about animals, you can add to the lists yourselves and create your own riddles. (Answers are on page 160.)

Animal Baby Names

Match the animal names to the baby animal names.

goat	colt
dog	calf
cat	kitten
horse	kid
chicken	chick
cow	cub
elephant	puppy
whale	owlet
pig	calf
lion	piglet
owl	calf

Animal Names and Homes

Match the animal names to the names of their homes.

fox	den
bee	web
lion	nest
bird	hive
spider	den

Animal Group Names

Match the animal names to the name of each group of animals.

cows	school
bees	pack
puppies/kittens	gaggle
wolves	pride
geese	swarm
fish	herd
ants	cloud
tadpoles	colony
lion	litter

Animals That Come from Eggs

Pick the animals that hatch from eggs.

chickens	snakes
ponguins	pigs
dogs	sharks
pigeons	octopuses
eagles	hummingbirds
whales	lizards
rats	crocodiles
turtles	frogs
tigers	ants
spiders	cats
ostriches	elephants

Animal Riddles

The perfect riddle for a preschooler is one in which information is given as a question, giving her the opportunity to answer correctly or at least make a good guess. (Answers are on page 160.)

I am the smallest bird, but I can move my wings faster than you can blink your eyes! I have a long, thin beak that is perfect for getting nectar out of flowers. What am I?

People call me "slimy," but really I'm smooth. I don't have any legs and I move around by curving my body on the ground. Sometimes I have pretty patterns on my skin. What am I?

I'm so small I will fit in your hand. I usually live on a farm. I am yellow and soft and make a peeping sound. I come out of an egg. What am I?

I am one of the largest animals on Earth. I have big, floppy ears, and I can spray water out of my trunk. What am I?

I am called the king of beasts because I make a loud roar. I keep my cubs safe in a den. I have soft fur, but don't try to touch it because I also have very sharp teeth! What am I?

I come from the largest egg of any animal. I have feathers, but I can't fly. I have a very long neck. What am I?

Pets

Having a pet is the perfect opportunity for children to experience nature in their own backyards. Dogs, cats, hamsters, parakeets, etc., will give you an opportunity to discuss habitat, food, and shelter of tame animals. Also, if you go back far enough in the animal lineage, your child can learn that even the family dog is related to wild animals. Be sure to introduce your youngster to the terms "wild" and "domestic" and to show him pictures from books and encyclopedias about your pet's ancestry.

Some animal names are listed below. Which ones would make good pets if you lived on a farm? in the city? in the suburbs? Which ones would never make good pets? Tell why. (Suggested answers are on page 160.)

parrot	tiger
cat	horse
pig	crocodile
hamster	monkey
snake	hippopotamus
dog	ostrich
hyena	rabbit
chicken	eagle
elephant	dinosaur

Where to Go

If you have a pet, start with a visit to its home. Show your child what you have done to make your pet more comfortable: shredded newspaper at the bottom of a rabbit cage, a pillow for the dog bed, or a sunning branch for a reptile aquarium. Compare these types of homes with the ones animals might have out in the wild. Ask your child if she thinks pets like being confined in cages or homes, or would they rather be free in the wild? Point out that there are advantages and disadvantages to each situation.

If you don't have a pet, or even if you do, you can visit a pet store to see a variety of animals. The employees are trained to know what makes a good pet home, so they will welcome your questions.

Veterinarians are experts on animals and, if you call ahead, your local vet may show you around his or her office. They are usually pleased to educate people about pets.

Animal shelters are suitable places to look for all types of potential pets. Call ahead to ask about their visiting hours, fees, and rules about pet adoptions. Most also give tours, which are intended to inform the public about animal neglect and maltreatment.

What to Do

Home Improvement

Have a family contest to see who can come up with the best (and most practical) idea to improve your pet's environment. Does your dog need a new blanket? Does your cat have a license? Does the bird cage need a thorough spring cleaning? Your pet is an important part of your family, so see how you can improve his or her home today.

Dictate a Letter

How would you feel if you were your family's pet? Have your child dictate a letter to you from the perspective of a pet. Have the pet talk about how much he enjoys being in your family. As he dictates, have him get into character by barking, meowing, or chirping. Have him report what types of changes he would like to see. Your child can sign the letter with a paw print or foot.

What Else?

A wonderful pet story, especially for city folks, is *Pet Show* by Jack Ezra Keats.

Ask silly questions like, "How would you keep a pet monkey from swinging all over your bedroom?"

Speaking of silly pets, read *Can I Keep Him?* by Steven Kellogg.

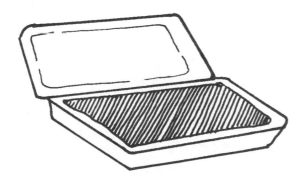

Dear Family:
I love being in this family. I love the walks and the family camping trips that I always get to go on. I love my bed. I only wish I could have steak for dinner every night!
Love
Maggie

Birds of a Feather

There is mystery in observing birds. Watching them fly makes you wonder how they do it. It looks impossible, yet they make it look so easy. In fact, humans were so envious of birds that we built flying machines. We also love to listen to birds twitter, chirp, peep, and whistle. Birds have personalities that are fun to watch—cocky robins, friendly chickadees, spooky owls. Much behavior is unique to birds, like begging with wide-open mouths and bathing with dirt, but birds are also capable of learned activities. A plastic or wooden owl is known to frighten away unsuspecting birds—until they realize that the owl never comes after them. You can build a child's natural curiosity about these animals by taking some special visits and doing one or more of the projects listed below.

Where to Go

If you have access to an aviary, perhaps within a nearby zoo, this would be a wonderful nature walk to experience with your child. Many aviaries have birds that are so tame they may land on you. Although your preschooler may be intimidated by being that close to nature, how fun would it be to see a bird sitting on mom or dad's head? Of course it is not a good idea to insist that your child enters an aviary if he or she seems frightened or the birds seem aggressive.

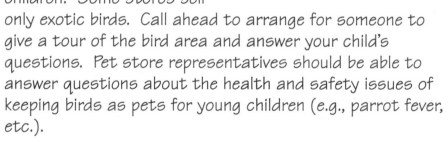

Pet stores are also a wonderful option for seeing smaller birds. Larger pet stores usually have cockatiels and parrots that are favorites of children. Some stores sell only exotic birds. Call ahead to arrange for someone to give a tour of the bird area and answer your child's questions. Pet store representatives should be able to answer questions about the health and safety issues of keeping birds as pets for young children (e.g., parrot fever, etc.).

Do you have a duck pond in a park near your home? Feeding the ducks is one of the earliest and fondest field trips for young children. Teach your little one how to tear off small bits of bread and toss them for the ducks to gobble. However, it is a good idea to check with a park official about the feeding policy. This is a sure winner!

Any forest or mountainous area is usually filled with the sounds of birds. When you walk in such areas, take along a field guide with colored pictures of birds. Binoculars are also a good idea, as birds in the wild are likely to keep their distance. Try imitating the variety of sounds you hear from different birds.

What to Do

Make a Milk Carton Bird Feeder

Your child will love sitting at a window and watching as the birds enjoy a special gift he's made for them.

Materials

- cardboard milk carton
- scissors
- string
- bird seed

Directions

Cut out the panels on two opposite sides of a clean milk carton. Poke a hole through the top and put a piece of string through the hole. Tie the string around a tree limb. Fill the bottom of the carton with bird seed and wait nearby for the birds to gather. You can decorate the bird feeder by painting it brown and adding sticks and leaves to make it look more natural. You must also keep the feeder full, as some birds may come to depend on it over time and may not survive without the feeder.

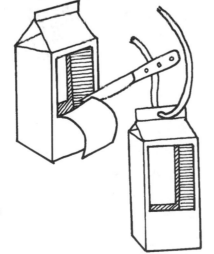

What Else?

Did you know that hummingbirds are attracted to the color red? If you have a hummingbird feeder, add a big red bow, but don't color the water with food coloring as it may make them ill.

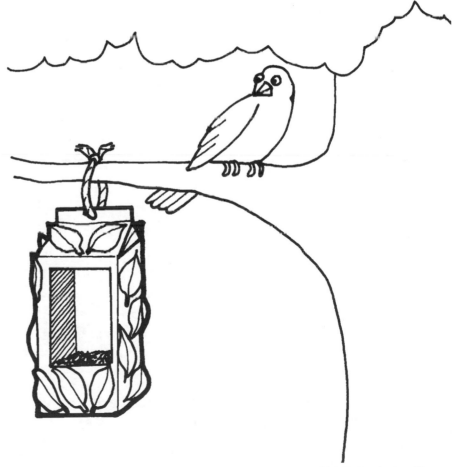

Create a Hand Print Peacock

This craft is a twist on the traditional project of using a hand as a brush to paint a turkey. It is also a little messy, but colorful and fun.

Materials

- brown, blue, green, and purple tempera paint
- large sheet of construction paper
- fine markers

Directions

Paint your child's thumb brown and her fingers and palm shades of blues, greens, and purples. Make a print of your child's hand on a piece of paper. After the print dries, decorate with facial features and a few thin plumes rising from the head.

Be a Bird

Have your child imitate different types of birds and their wing movements: hawks with a large, sweeping motion of the arms; hummingbirds with vigorous arm swings; penguins with arms against her sides and hands pointing out.

What Else?

An all-time favorite children's classic is Robert McCloskey's *Make Way for Ducklings*.

Make a Bird Caller

If your little one hasn't mastered the art of whistling, give this easy-to-make bird-caller a try.

Place a long, wide piece of grass between two craft or Popsicle sticks. Wrap one end with a rubber band. Hold it to your mouth lengthwise, and close the other end with your thumb and index finger. Blow, making harmonica-type sounds. How long does it take for a bird to respond?

Help the Birds Build Their Homes

You can actually help your neighborhood birds build their nests with supplies found around your house. Toward the end of winter, prepare a shallow container with some of the following supplies: snips of colored yarn, thread, or string; pieces of shredded newspaper; cotton balls; small pieces of fabric strips; and pieces of lace, rickrack, and fringe. Leave in the yard. Perhaps you and your child can think of more colorful and comfortable items to feather a nest. Your neighborhood birds will make the most colorful nests in town.

Duck Feather Experiment

When your preschooler watches ducks and asks how their feathers stay dry, you'll be ready with a hands-on way to show her.

Materials

- feathers, either collected or store-bought
- small piece of canvas
- vegetable oil
- pastry brush
- glue

Directions

Glue or staple some store-bought or collected feathers onto a piece of canvas. Brush on some vegetable oil with a pastry brush; dab off the excess. Pour some water over the treated feathers. Does the water stick or just slide off? Ducks have a special chemical that helps protect their feathers from the water, just like the chemical you used on your feathers.

What Else?

Do you remember this song from your childhood days?

Oh it's gonna be a long winter.

And what will the birds do then,

The poor things.

They'll fly to the south

To keep their heads warm

And tuck their heads under their wings,

The poor things.

Wild Animals

Although we usually think of wild animals as having large teeth and ferocious growls, any animal can be considered wild simply because of where it lives. Most of us have to visit special places to find wild animals, but don't forget the obvious creatures that show up in your backyard.

Animals that you may see can be placed into one of the following categories: mammals (skunks, raccoons, possums), birds (ducks, robins, bluebirds), rodents (mice, rats), and reptiles (snakes, frogs, lizards). Depending on where you live and the types of areas where you walk, you can see a variety of these animals. Ask your child what his favorite animals are and which one he would like to be.

The most important thing to remember about wild animals is that they are not pets and are never to be touched. Emphasize to your child that he or she is never to touch an animal in the wild, living or dead.

Where to Go

There are some animals that you will not be able to see in their natural habitats. Zoos, wildlife preserves, and nature centers will provide an opportunity for you to show your child what life is like for these animals without buying plane tickets to the rain forest or the polar ice caps.

Zoos have become wonderful centers of education about animals. Perhaps your local zoo, even if not in a metropolis, will have classes for children on weekends and during the summer. Larger zoos also have animal nurseries, a must-see for young children who are always enamored with anything associated with babies. Be sensitive if your child has a fear of a certain type of animal, but if he or she is willing, this is the time to become better acquainted with snakes, bears, or elephants.

Wild animal parks are unique opportunities to see animals interact as they would in the wild. Instead of being constricted by cages or glass enclosures, animals roam as they would in their natural homes. If your child has a special interest in an animal that can be found at a wild animal park, a trip there will make a great adventure. Let your child know that she will not be able to get as close to animals in the animal park as she can at the zoo, so that she understands what she will be seeing and is not disappointed.

What to Do

Animal Coverings Hunt

Animal-inspired fabric coverings may not be the real thing, but they will show your child that animals feel different from each other.

Materials

A variety of fabrics including the following:

- thick and furry (bear)
- scaly (fish)
- leathery (elephant)
- suede (cow)
- animal-printed fabrics
- zebra and tiger stripes
- leopard ocelot spots
- brown paper bag
- list of animals to match the fabric samples

Directions

Place the fabric samples in the bag without letting your child see them. Tell the child you are going to go on a hunt for some different animals. Say something like, "Without looking, I want you to put your hand in the bag and hunt for a cow." After your child finishes laughing, have him or her put the hand in and feel around for what she thinks a cow would feel like. Do this for your whole list of animals and fabrics. Chances are, your child will have some good animal suggestions for some of the fabrics, as well.

What Else?

Read *The Mixed-up Chameleon* by Eric Carle, and then make your own mixed-up animals with magazine cutouts.

Play Animal Charades

There's nothing more fun to a kid than pretending he or she is an animal. Find and cut magazine photos of animals and place them in a box. You and your child can take turns pulling pictures from the box and acting them out for each other. If silent movements aren't enough, a wild animal sound can be a good hint.

Walking with Antlers

This activity will give your child some appreciation for what some animals experience.

Demonstrate how to spread your hands to look like antlers and hold them to your head to make small antlers. Then, to make big adult antlers, give your child a yard stick and have him hold it on his head with the ends sticking out. While you observe him carefully to be sure that he doesn't endanger himself, have him walk around the house and outside. How will he get through doorways? past bushes? Being a moose must be hard!

What Else?

When you run out of your own animal sounds, try *Hoot, Howl, Hiss* by Michelle Koch.

Nancy Tafuri's detailed illustrations in *I Love You, Little One* are so brilliant that they are almost like looking at live animals.

Make a Raccoon Mask

This quick and easy mask will bring out your child's wild side.

Materials

- paper plate, cut in half
- scissors (for adult use)
- hole punch
- string
- black and brown markers

Directions

Use the scissors to cut out eye holes and a space for the nose. Punch holes on each side of the plate, and tie the string to fit the mask around your child's head. Show your child how to color circles around the eye holes to look like a raccoon.

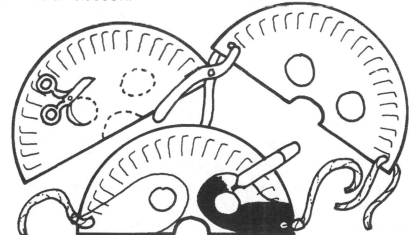

What Else?

How many stories can you think of where the fox was a bad guy? "Chicken Little," "Jemima Puddleduck," and "The Gingerbread Man" are a few. Have a discussion with your child about whether or not the fox is always a bad animal when found in nature.

Play Possum Tag

This is a variation of freeze tag. Choose who is "it" and who is "possum." "It" chases the possum until the possum is tagged. The tagged player then plays possum by freezing in position while "it" counts to 10. If "it" sees possum move during that 10-second time period, the possum becomes "it" and "it" becomes the possum. If not, start the chase all over again.

Go on an Animal Scavenger Hunt

Prior to a visit to a zoo or wild animal park, prepare a list of characteristics to find. Some examples would include the following:

- Find an animal with brown fur.
- Find an animal with three colors of feathers.
- Find an animal that sleeps at night.
- Make up characteristics that would apply to more than one animal.

What Else?

Find a copy of the Caldecott winner *The Beastly Feast* by Clair Lent; it is a fun rhyming book with an assortment of exotic animals. You might also enjoy the rhymes found in Nancy White Carlstrom's *What Would You Do If You Lived at the Zoo?*

Create Plaster of Paris Paw Prints

If you are fortunate enough to come into contact with some real deer, bear, or coyote prints, you might want to save them as proof.

Materials

- plaster of Paris
- water

Directions

Follow the instructions on the package for mixing plaster of Paris with water to get the consistency of cake batter. Dig a little ditch around the print. Pour the mixture into the print until it is completely covered and the mixture flows into the ditch. When the plaster is completely dry, lift it out, brush it off, and you will have a perfect print of the paw.

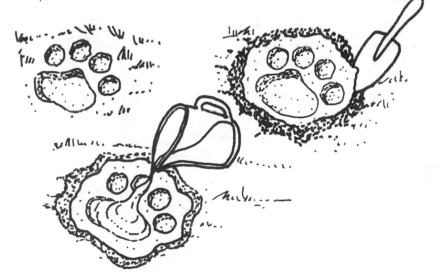

What Else?

Did you know that the Teddy bear is actually named after President Teddy Roosevelt. Legend has it that although Roosevelt was a great hunter, he would not kill a baby bear cub. Soon after that information became known, the first Teddy bear was made and named after him.

Read *A House Is a House for Me* by Mary Ann Hoberman for a very different look at habitats.

Coloring Snake Patterns

Snakes are easy and fun subjects for art. Draw a large curvy or coiled snake outline and put a simple design on it: stripes, diamonds circles, etc. If you want it to be realistic, have an encyclopedia or nature guide available as you draw. Crayons and colored markers are usually the best material for preschoolers, but if you want to try something different, watercolors would also be pretty.

What Else?

When a snake sticks its tongue out at you, it's not teasing—it's smelling you. Snakes use their tongues to pick up dangerous scents around them.

Be a Marsupial Mom

Children love to pretend being parents. With the help of some items around the house, your child can be a marsupial mama or a possum papa.

Explain to your child that some animal babies are born and can walk around a few hours later, like horses or chicks. Some animals, though, must be held close to their moms until they can grow to be strong and safe on their own. Some baby animals, like kangaroos or possums, get to live inside their mom's special pocket.

Tell your child that when a baby possum is born, it is about the size of a raisin. Give your child a raisin to carry in his pocket and take care of all day. (Be sure to remember to check those pockets before they go in the wash!) Next, have your child carry a small stuffed animal on her head or sticking out of the back of her shirt collar everywhere she goes. This is what the mama possum does. If your child has clothes with a large front pocket, the animal can poke out of that for the day's adventures. Boys can pretend to be possum papas, but in reality, the male possum leaves after mating and male kangaroos do not have pouches. How long can your little one be a good kangaroo or possum parent?

What Else?

Compare habitats by reading Jan Brett's version of the classic tale, *The City Mouse and the Country Mouse.*

Paw Print Page

Copy this page and take it with you on nature walks. See how many of the prints you can find in the dirt, mud, or sand.

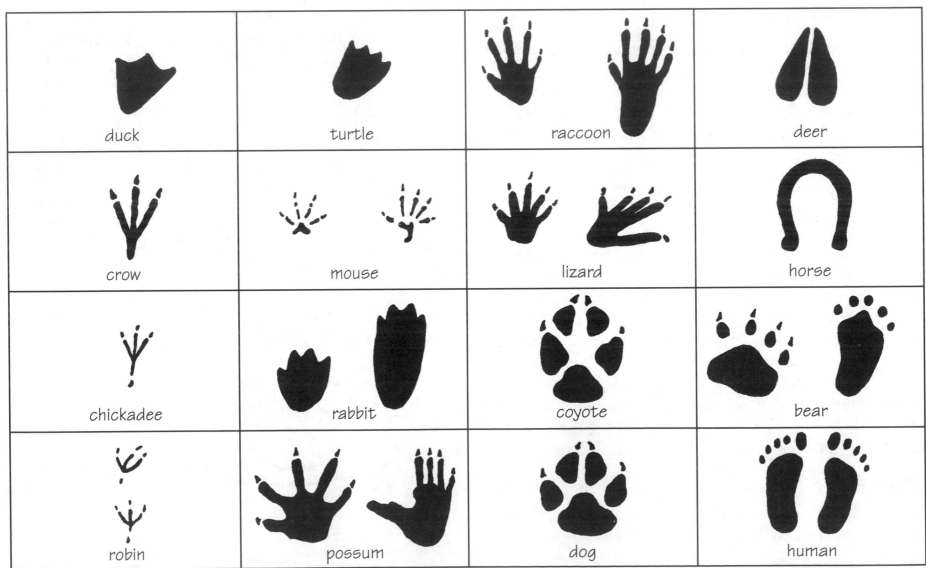

duck	turtle	raccoon	deer
crow	mouse	lizard	horse
chickadee	rabbit	coyote	bear
robin	possum	dog	human

Farm Animals

Unless you have a dog or cat, farm animals are often the first animals with which young children have contact. In fact, some children's first words are imitations of animal sounds. There are also many children's books and board books with farm animal themes.

Unlike other animal situations, animals on the farm are workers. Cows provide milk, pigs become pork, and horses and oxen pull equipment. Even dogs work by herding sheep or cattle. Ask your child if he thinks the animals enjoy their jobs or would they rather just be pets. What animal does he think is most important on the farm?

Where to Go

A farm, dairy, or ranch is the best place to enjoy farm animals and their environment. Commercial farms and dairies are often set up to give tours.

If you do not live near a farm, the next best option is a petting zoo. These wonderful centers provide opportunities for your child to see, touch, and feed barnyard animals like chickens, goats, pigs, and cows. Every child needs the opportunity to see live animals. It is exciting to hear the animals' different noises and to smell their distinctive scents—well, maybe that's not the best part of farm life!

What to Do

Make Butter

You can have homemade butter, just like people did 100 years ago.

Materials

- baby food jar
- clean glass marble
- heavy cream
- crackers

Directions

Fill a clean baby food jar about halfway with cream. Add the marble. Shake, shake, shake until you can see the consistency of the cream changing to a solid. When it becomes butter, you can spread it on crackers for a yummy treat.

Milk a Surgical Glove

If you don't have a cow nearby, this is a great substitute. With a pin, poke a small hole in the thumb and index finger of a surgical glove. Fill the glove with milk and close the top with a twist tie. As you hold the "udder," let your child milk it into his mouth. He may never complain about drinking milk again!

What Else?

How many different foods and items can you name that come from pigs?

Don't forget to sing the old favorite, "Old MacDonald Had a Farm."

Eggs

Which came first, the chicken or the egg? You may think the answer is elusive, but just ask your preschooler—they often have strong opinions on issues like this. In the life cycles of animals and insects, eggs are the beginning of life. Although fertilization is probably beyond the mind of a preschooler, there are some wonderful facts you can share about eggs and the babies in them that will make your little one feel very smart.

- Most animals have what is known as an "egg tooth", which helps them peck away at the inside of the egg and eventually push their way out. Soon after hatching, the egg tooth falls out, since it is no longer needed.

   The first tiny peck in an egg that causes a crack is called a pip.

- Eggs come in all sizes and many different colors, but they also come in different consistencies. Snakes have very soft, pliable eggs, while frogs and some fish have translucent eggs.

Investigating eggs does not stop with the outside package. The experience isn't complete until you and your child have seen a baby chick (or some other animal) actually emerge after hours of hard work from their first home.

Ask your little one what she thinks it feels like to be inside an egg, trying to get out. If you feel it is appropriate, you can mention the parallels between animals in eggs and a child growing inside of its mother as she prepares to be born.

Where to Go

Most zoos have hatcheries or at least opportunities to show off their unhatched babies. Call ahead to find out what season or month they anticipate the most egg activity.

Even more fun is a real hatchery, where you can watch chicks hatch in incubators. Some hatcheries give tours, and some even let children hold the newborn chicks in their hands. Don't forget your camera.

Of course, a farm is a wonderful place to see animals come to life. If you have access to one, you will be fortunate enough to see not only chicks, but their parents as well. While you are at the farm, be sure to point out which animals hatch from eggs and which animals are born live.

What to Do

Play Guess Who?

Using the list of animals on page 43, look for and cut out pictures in magazines of animals that hatch from eggs. Put each picture in a plastic colored egg like those used to hold treats for Easter. Once the eggs are filled, take turns with your child choosing and acting out the animals found inside the eggs. At first, try demonstrating the animals' actions without sounds; use sounds as hints when actions don't provide enough of a clue.

What Else?

If you do not have access to eggs that you can watch hatch, a beautiful substitute is the Eyewitness Series book *Eggs*.

What animal has the biggest egg? An ostrich!

Decorate Eggs the Natural Way

It doesn't have to be Easter to decorate eggs the way they did it in the old days.

Materials

- coffee grounds
- carrots
- beets or any plant that has strong color
- saucepans
- hard-boiled eggs
- egg cartons

Directions

Prepare the dyes by cooking the food items in separate pots and straining out the food. (This is to be done by an adult only.) Place the hard-boiled eggs into the food dyes, and let them sit as long as you like. The longer the eggs sit, the stronger the color will be, although the color will never be as dark as commercially-prepared dyes. Remove the eggs with tongs or a spoon and place them in an egg carton to dry.

Play Life Cycle Concentration

Copy this page onto heavy white paper. Color the pictures, if you like. Show your child the cards in the correct order for each animals' life cycle. When the child has a good grasp of how the cards go together, mix them up, turn them upside down, and take turns with the child trying to find all four of each animal's life cycle cards. If this is a new concept for your child, be sure to give lots of help and encouragement!

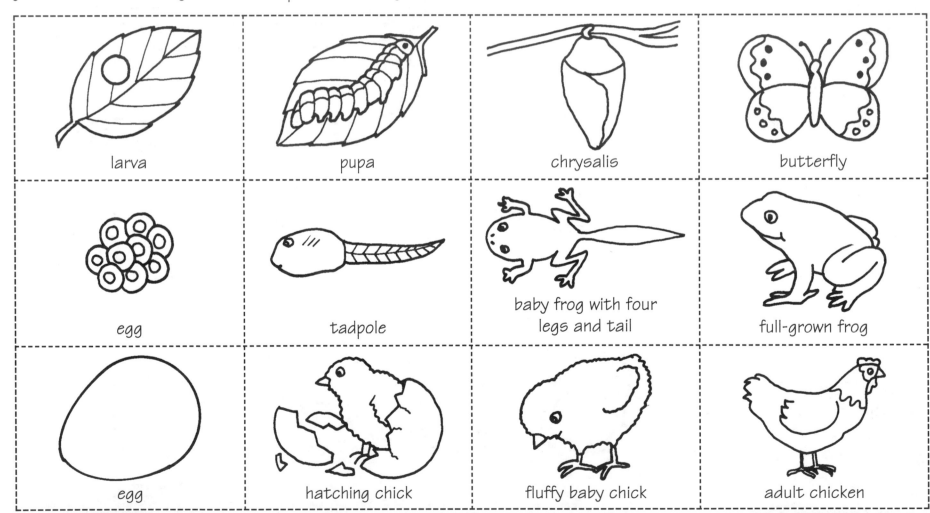

| larva | pupa | chrysalis | butterfly |

| egg | tadpole | baby frog with four legs and tail | full-grown frog |

| egg | hatching chick | fluffy baby chick | adult chicken |

Insects, Bugs, and Creepy Crawlies

"Bugs are yucky!" Is what most young children say when they first encounter them. But bugs aren't bad, and if we give children a chance to take a good look at them without prejudice, our children can become fearless bug scientists, or entomologists.

Insects are classified into the animal grouping arthropod. This means they have jointed legs, an exoskeleton, and no backbone. All insects have six legs and most have wings. Insects have three body parts: the head, the abdomen, and the thorax. Bugs are what we loosely call the rest of the insect kingdom. The difference between insects and the rest of these creepy crawlies is not in function but appearance. Spiders, or arachnids, have eight legs and no wings. Worms have no legs at all. Millipedes often have hundreds of legs, and centipedes, their more dangerous counterparts, have bodies made of many tiny segments. Snails and slugs, garden inhabitants, do not have the characteristics to be bugs.

Although it is sometimes hard to believe, we have much to be thankful for when it comes to insects and other bugs. They provide nourishment for much of the animal kingdom; they help to pollinate flowers; and many eat decayed matter. Despite their appearance, they are helpers in our world.

Where to Go

The best place to see bugs—fortunately or unfortunately—is probably in your own backyard. With a tape measure, show your child how to measure earthworms or ant trails. Get out a spoon and magnifying glass and start investigating the inhabitants of your plants such as aphids and grasshoppers.

Some pet stores have exotic pets like tarantulas. Call around in your area to see if you can find exotic cockroaches or millipedes.

If there is a nature center within driving distance, you will find it is a wonderful resource to visit. One thing they may have is a display of insects and arthropods. Call before you go to find out what they have and prepare your child for what will be seen. Nature centers have trained staff who may allow your child to hold the creepy crawlies. (You want a chance, too, don't you?)

There are a number of butterfly sanctuaries in the United States where you have a special opportunity to see hundreds of live butterflies up close in a habitat created for them to live and for you to see. Your local library, zoo, or natural history museum should have information on where to find such a setting.

What to Do

Make Your Own Bug House

For an up-close look at bugs, there is nothing like a cozy bug house.

Materials

- jar with metal lid
- duct tape
- screen cut to fit lid
- dirt

Directions

Poke holes in the metal lid of a glass jar and tape the screen to the underside of the lid. Before catching a bug, add a couple of scoops of dirt and a small branch. Once you catch a bug, place it in its new home and add a little of whatever plant it was munching. Bug houses are great for up-close observation, but try to let the bug loose before it dies.

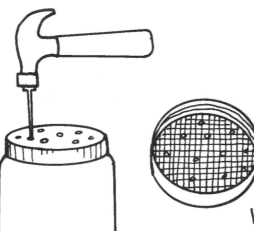

What Else?

You can have your own butterflies to send out into the world. There are commercially-made products available in toy and science specialty stores or through nature catalogs that will help you raise live butterfly larvae at home. See page 157 for resources.

Make an Egg Carton Caterpillar

This standard craft is easy to make and full of personality.

Materials

- cardboard egg carton
- green tempera paint
- brush
- wiggle eyes
- colored pipe cleaners
- scissors
- glue

Directions

Cut the egg carton down to one strip of six egg cups. Paint the carton green. Add other colors for stripes or polka dots as desired. When it is dry, glue on the eyes and poke pipe cleaners in as antennae, curling them at the ends. Does this look like any of the caterpillars in your yard?

Fingerprint Ants

With a red or black stamp pad, ink the pad of your index finger and stamp it on the paper. Make a second print near it, just connected to the first print. With your pinkie fingertip, ink and print a tiny head. This will show the three body parts of an ant. Don't forget to add antennae. Can you make an ant trail? Draw an ice cream cone at the end—isn't that where you would go if you were an ant?

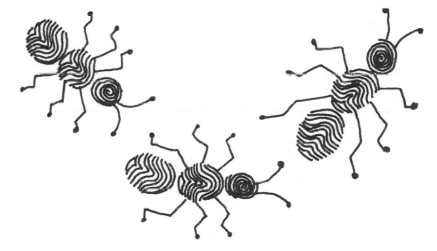

What Else?

What happens when you interrupt a trail of ants? Count how many seconds it takes them to regroup.

Buy an ant farm at a toy or educational supply store. Be sure not to mix ants from different colonies, as they'll fight to the death. Try to include a queen ant.

Make a Worm House

In this special worm house, you can see the tunnels appear before your eyes.

Materials

- glass jar with lid
- lettuce leaves
- dirt
- soil
- black construction paper

Directions

Fill the jar with soil up to the last three inches. Add a couple of lettuce leaves. Poke holes in the lid for air. Tape a piece of black paper around the glass. Add a few worms from your garden. They are easy to find; look in moist areas early in the morning. After a couple of hours, tear off the black paper and see what kinds of tunnels the worms have formed. Explain to your child that this is just what worms do in the wild and that the tunneling helps break up the soil. When you are done with your worms, return them to their garden home.

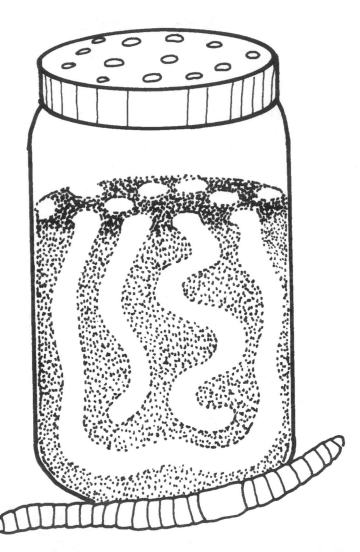

What Else?

Read *Two Bad Ants* by Chris Van Allsberg. What things in this story could really happen? What things are fiction?

Make a Butterfly

This is an easy, colorful craft that looks pretty when hung in a window.

Materials

- coffee filters
- pipe cleaners
- eye dropper
- diluted food coloring or liquid watercolor paints

Directions

Using the eye dropper, dribble paint or food coloring onto the coffee filter. The color will spread across the entire filter. When the filter is dry, gather it in the middle with a pipe cleaner. Form the ends of the pipe cleaner as antennae. Hang your pretty insect in the window!

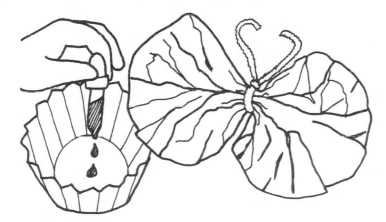

What Else?

The Very Hungry Caterpillar by Eric Carle is a must for any preschool discussion on caterpillars and butterflies.

Circular Ladybugs

Ladybugs lend themselves beautifully to an introduction to the circle shape.

Materials

- large black circle
- slightly smaller red circle
- glue stick
- many small black circles
- blunt scissors
- two hole-punched red circles

Directions

The large black circle is the ladybug's body. Cut the red circle in half and glue the two pieces over the black circle as wings. Glue the smaller black circles over the red wings. Finally, add the two tiny circles as eyes. As you do this activity, emphasize the circle shape each time you use it.

Save the Spiders

Spiders are creepy crawlies with a special mission and some unique qualities not found in other bugs. Like insects, spiders are classified as *arthropods*, meaning they have jointed legs, an exoskeleton, and no backbone. What differentiates them from insects are their four pairs of legs and two body parts—the cephalothorax (head and thorax combined) and the abdomen.

Spiders are widely reputed as great weavers. While some spiders have ornate and patterned webs, other webs look like just a mess of dusty silk. Whatever the shape, weaving is accomplished with the aid of the spider's unique silk glands and spinerets. The spinning, which looks like an insect art form, is merely an instinct of spider behavior to create their homes and traps. We should appreciate the work of the spider, as their main benefit to us is reduction of the pest population.

Surprisingly, only a few spider species are harmful to humans. Black widows, common in North America, are easily distinguished by their bulb-like bodies and red hour-glass shape on their underside. Brown recluse spiders are another poisonous species; they cause a welt that may last for a couple of weeks. These spiders are usually not deadly, though, and the vast majority of spiders are completely harmless to humans. Although spiders may not be pretty, it is a good idea to help your child see them for what they are—household and garden helpers.

Look for these symptoms if you suspect a spider bite: fever and severe pains in stomach, muscles, and feet. These symptoms may last for days. Although uncomfortable, very few spider bites are fatal. Still, it is a good idea to get to an emergency room for a doctor's evaluation, if you see any suspect symptoms.

Where to Go

It is easy to search for spiders in your own home and garden. Look at the activities on the pages that follow to see how you can make the best of a creepy crawly adventure.

If your local pet store carries exotic pets, see if they have displays of tarantulas. These spiders are not poisonous, although they are furry and frightening. Although rare, tarantulas are capable of throwing stickers from their legs into an observer's eyes, so do keep your distance.

Call your nearest nature center or natural science museum about displays of spiders.

What to Do

Save a Spider Web

This is a fun way to have a closer look at a spider's masterpiece.

Materials

- black or blue construction paper
- hair spray

Directions

If you find an intact, abandoned spider web, you can save it onto a piece of black or dark blue construction paper. Spray the paper with hair spray, place the paper behind the web, and draw it toward you. This will release the web and transfer it to your paper. This is a wonderful hands-on experience for young children, but it is not a good idea to use it often. Spiders sometimes eat their old webs. Don't take away your friendly backyard spider's snack.

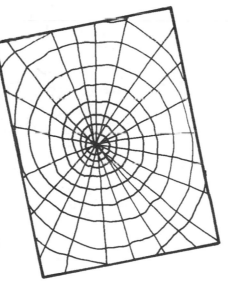

Make Your Own Cobweb

Your child will love creating a web design that takes over an entire room. Most people can find a cobweb somewhere in their house. See if you can spot one, and before you dust it away, show it to your child. Then hand him a ball of string, tie one end to a bedpost or doorknob and let him go at it, spinning a cobweb across the room. There does not need to be any design or pattern. Wrapping, spinning, and attaching will keep your little spider occupied for a morning. The only question at the end of the activity will be "How do I get out of here?"

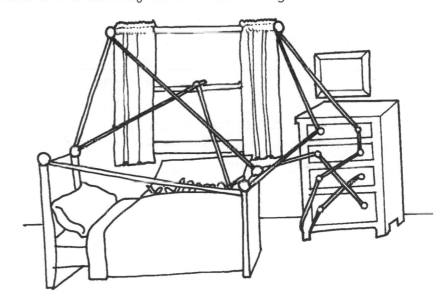

What Else?

With its tactile pages, *The Very Busy Spider* by Eric Carle, is a friendly introduction to preschool study on spiders.

Make a Paper Plate Spider

Most spiders are friendly. You might even give this one a name.

Materials

- paper plate
- black tempera paint
- paint brushes
- yellow tempera paint
- stapler
- string or dental floss
- black construction paper strips for legs

Directions

Paint the paper plate black. While waiting for it to dry, accordion fold the eight strips of black paper that will becomes it legs. Then paint two small yellow eyes at the rim of any part of the plate. Staple four legs on one side and four on the other, making sure that the eyes you have painted become the front of the spider. Poke a hole at the top, and knot the string underneath the spider. Hang your friendly companion from a ceiling.

What Else?

Although your little one may be too young to listen to the book *Charlotte's Web* by E. B. White, he or she may find the video version entertaining. Check with your library to see if they have a copy you can borrow, or rent it from your local video store.

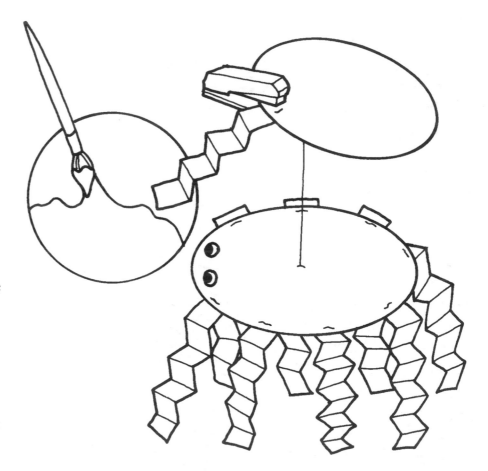

Act Out Spider Rhymes

To a preschooler, there's nothing like pretending. Act out preschool favorites like "Little Miss Muffet" and "Itsy Bitsy Spider." Take turns being the spider. What props can you find in the kitchen to make the rhyme into a play?

Little Miss Muffet

Little Miss Muffet sat on a
    tuffet,
Eating her curds and whey;
Along came a spider
who sat down beside her
And frightened Miss Muffet
    away.

Itsy Bitsy Spider

Itsy Bitsy Spider
Climbing up the spout;
Down came the rain
And washed the spider out;
Out came the sunshine
And dried up all the rain;
Itsy Bitsy spider
Climbing up again.

Make a Black Widow Danger Sign

Putting this special sign in the yard will be a good reminder to children about watching out for these spiders. Although most spiders are safe and even helpful, there are some that are very dangerous. Copy this page onto construction paper and have your child color the body black and the hour-glass shape red. Cut out the shape and glue it onto a craft stick or other sturdy stick. Poke this sign into the ground or tape it to a garage wall at children's eye level anywhere you think your little one might see a dangerous spider.

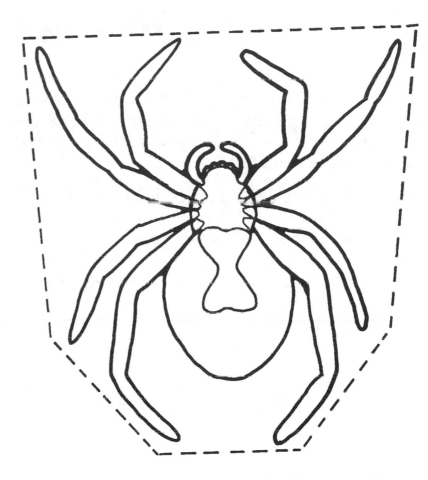

What Else?

There are many stories of the tricky little spider Anasi in African folklore. Ask your librarian to help you choose one that would be appropriate for your preschooler.

Walking Among Rocks

Unless you are looking at the Grand Canyon, rocks are perhaps the least glamorous aspect of nature. Without them, though, we would have no mountains, no volcanoes, and no sand on the beach. Also, many rocks are actually crystals that are beautiful to look at.

As you walk with your child, you may see both boulders and pebbles. You may see layers of compressed rock in mountainsides that developed over millions of years. You might even have the opportunity to see volcanoes or caves. The formation of all of these things are infinity to the mind of preschoolers. How can they take in something so awesome that has taken millions of years to develop and is still changing today?

Rocks, mountains, and hillside erosion are perfect ways to introduce how the world has changed over time and is continuing to change. In fact, many natural disasters that occur affect mountains and rock formations. That is what makes them so interesting to look at. Volcanic lava makes rocks, earthquakes rearrange the shapes of continents, and wildfires burn away trees and allow new vegetation to fill in the earth.

Teaching our children not to fear nature is a responsibility of parents. Hopefully, however, your family won't be in the vicinity when any of these catastrophes are happening. Though we are unable to control everything that happens, we can try to understand it. Disaster can become awe-invoking instead of an object of fear and uncertainty.

Standing on Rocky Ground

Anywhere you take a walk, you will notice rocks around you. Your toddler may notice them long before you do. Rocks seem so permanent. Before there were people, there were rocks. Before dinosaurs roamed the Earth, there were rocks. Before anything could grow, there were rocks. They have always been a stable force in nature.

All rocks have multiple elements and can be classified into one of three groups: igneous, sedimentary, and metamorphic. Igneous rocks are actually cooled magma (or lava) on the interior or exterior of the Earth. Usually igneous rocks have a lot of texture. Granite, obsidian, and basalt are types of igneous rock. Sedimentary rocks are usually the easiest to recognize. They usually are striped, which shows the layers of sediment that have been squeezed together to form the rock. The layers in sedimentary stone are sometimes visible on hillsides that have been cut away or eroded. Lastly, metamorphic rocks are rocks that were previously igneous or sedimentary but were changed by extreme heat and pressure and time to produce a new substance. For instance, limestone, a sedimentary rock, turns into marble when it has been exposed to extreme temperatures and pressure over thousands of years.

The prettiest stones are gems or crystals because they usually consist of bright colors, shiny surfaces, and prismatic shapes. These are not rocks since they are made up of only a single element. Diamonds, for instance, are made solely of carbon. Emeralds, amethyst, and even salt and sugar crystals are each made up of a single element.

Where to Go

Riverbeds provide a wonderful supply of naturally-tumbled stones. If you inspect these rocks you will notice wonderful differences in their colors, textures, and shapes.

If you are fortunate enough to live in or visit the Southwestern states, be sure to point out the interesting shapes of the mountains and rocks, not to mention the colors and sediment levels. There is not another place on our Earth that has rock forms like these.

To find a variety of really interesting rocks and minerals, visit a nature store or gemologist shop. They will carry both rough stones and stones tumbled smooth in a variety of shapes and colors. You can talk about which ones look similar. Most of these stones are relatively inexpensive, which is nice as your child will inevitably want to start collecting them once you show them to him or her. Help your child decorate a small box to hold this collection of treasures.

What to Do

Collect and Classify Rocks

Sorting and classifying rocks is a perfect preschool activity. As you walk, allow your child to collect any rocks he or she likes. A small plastic bucket is perfect for carrying them. When you return home, show your child how to sort the rocks by different attributes into an egg container (page 152). For classifying, use adjectives like "bumpy," "smooth," "large," "small," "shiny," and "dull." Use color words as well. Set similarly colored rocks (grey, for instance) in a line from lightest to darkest.

Make Edible Rocks

Rock candy is easy to make and yummy to eat.

Materials

- saucepan
- 1 cup water
- 2 cups sugar
- Pyrex measuring cup
- clean string
- pencil

Directions

An adult can boil the water on the stove. Pour in the sugar and stir until the sugar dissolves. When the mixture has cooled, pour it into the Pyrex cup. Tie a piece of string to the middle of a pencil. Balance the pencil on the measuring cup so that the string dangles into the sugar water. It will take a few days before the sugar crystals start to form onto the string. When they look good and chunky, eat the crystals.

Create Stone Bugs

These stone bugs make nice paperweights for gift giving.

Materials

- small rocks
- wiggle eyes
- tempera paint
- white glue

Directions

Find some small rocks in your garden or on your walks that have a smooth texture and rounded shape. Paint the rock a foundation color (red for a ladybug, yellow for a bee, for example) and use black paint for an accent color. When the paint has dried, add wiggle eyes. Soon you can have a shelf full of friendly bugs.

(**Note:** These bugs are safest and happiest indoors, where their pretty colors won't wash off.)

What Else?

How many words can you think of that rhyme with "rocks?" Can you make a silly sentence out of them?

Make a Crystal Garden

Because of the odor from the ammonia, do this colorful and easy experiment outside. You can find laundry bluing in the detergent aisle of the grocery store.

Materials

- small plastic cup
- 3 tablespoons laundry bluing
- 3 tablespoons water
- 3 tablespoons ammonia
- 2 tablespoons salt
- liquid food coloring
- charcoal

Directions

Mix the ingredients until the salt is dissolved. Put a couple of pieces of charcoal in the cup and pour the liquid mixture over it. Squeeze a few drops of food coloring over the solution. Watch over the next 24 hours to see the crystals appear.

What Else?

Rock Collecting by Roma Gans is a good children's book on finding, identifying, and collecting rocks and minerals.

Bake and Eat Rock Replicas

Use this delicious demonstration, and pretend you are geologists breaking rocks apart to see what they contain.

Materials

- your favorite chocolate chip cookie recipe
- candy coated chocolates
- nuts
- coconut
- raisins
- toothpicks
- baking utensils

Directions

As you mix your cookie dough, add spoonfuls of the rest of the ingredients. Don't overbake these cookies. After the cookies cool, give your child a couple to investigate. Explain that geologists have to break apart rocks to see what is inside. Can she break apart her cookie to see what elements it contains? Have her use the toothpicks to carefully pull apart the different pieces of cookie in little piles. Of course, when you are all done, these rocks are great to eat. You can't say that about the rocks geologists work on!

Dirt, Mud, and Layers of Earth

Dirt looks brown and boring, unless you are a preschooler. From sandcastles to mud pies, dirt is a staple of childhood play. Parents are often reluctant to let their little ones get dirty, but remember that dirt is a creative tool with which children can learn many things—from building roads and digging holes to making gooey mud desserts. The various textures of the dirt are a valuable tactile experience, so don't be afraid to let your little one dig in the dirt.

"What is under all that dirt?" might be a good question to start with as you observe your preschooler digging. The Earth is made up of layers. The crust, which is the outside layer of solid rock, is the thinnest layer—only about 40 miles at its thickest point. The crust consists of all of the mountains, volcanoes, rocks, and continents—all land masses. As archaeologists have dug deeper into the crust, more and more fossils have been discovered. Children find fossils fascinating, and the bigger, the better.

If you were drilling to the next layer, which no one has yet done, you would reach the mantel, a much thicker layer of hot rock. Last is the core. The outer core is extremely hot, liquid metal. The inner core is so hot and compressed that it is actually solid. It is the hottest part of our planet.

Where to Go

Your own backyard after a good rain is the best place to make mud pies and experience the consistency of mud. Wear a good rain slicker and old pair of sneakers, be prepared with a few sand toys and play trucks, and you and your child can play happily for hours in the slippery, gooshy mess.

The Southwestern states are wonderful for showing the layers of rock that have formed over time. These are all in the top layer of our earth—the crust—but for children to see the layers of sedimentation that has formed helps to give them an idea of what the Earth's layers must be like.

Natural history museums often have exhibits of fossils and dinosaur bones, and exhibits that show the age and changes of our Earth. For your child, at his age, it is enough just to allow him to gawk at the size of some prehistoric creatures.

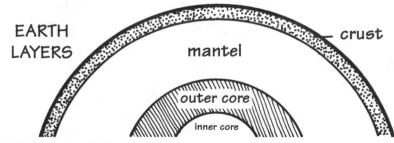

EARTH LAYERS — crust / mantel / outer core / inner core

What to Do

Make Clean Mud

Does clean mud sound too good to be true? Give this recipe a try.

Materials

- 6 rolls of white toilet paper
- water to cover
- 2 small bars of Ivory soap, grated
- 1½ cups borax powder

Directions

Unroll the toilet paper in a large tub and cover with water. Let it soak for 2–3 days. Squeeze the water out of the toilet paper, add the grated soap and borax, and knead soap together. The more this substance is played with, the better it gets blended. Cover it each night, and it will last for weeks. Play with clean mud as you would "dirty" mud—make mud pies and feel for all-around gooshiness. The clean-up, of course, will be a breeze.

Go on a Fossil Hunt

This is an easy fossil hunt that is guaranteed to be a success.

Materials

- bones (see note below)
- small plastic sieve
- other items for digging
- plastic washtub
- sand
- spoons

Directions

For this experience, you can use either plastic bones purchased at a nature store or clean chicken bones. (If using chicken bones, wash with bleach and dry completely before using.) Hide the bones in a sand box or plastic washtub filled with sand. Using small sieves and spoons, remove the bones. You might find you have a future paleontologist in your family.

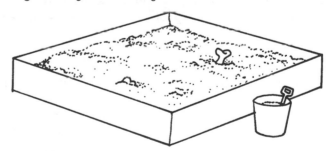

What Else?

Muddigush by Kimberly Knutson is a very descriptive book that is perfect for pre-mud play.

Be a Scientist

How do scientists know what is inside the Earth? Here's a demonstration where your little one can be a geologist.

Materials

- box with a lid
- ball

Directions

Without your child's knowledge, put a ball inside a box and cover it with a lid. Call in your child and tell him that he is going to be a scientist. Scientists ask questions and try to figure out answers. The first question you might ask your child is, what is inside the box? How would you know? What are some different ways you could solve this riddle? After some discussion, encourage your child to shake the box. Now what can he tell you? Finally, let him open the box. After you have had some time to play with the ball together, ask him what is inside the earth. How does he know? How do scientists know? Can they shake the Earth? What kinds of tests does your child think scientists do to understand the inside of the Earth?

Make Cupcake Earth Layers

Become a geologist with a colorful demonstration that your child will remember for a long time.

Materials

- white or yellow cake mix and ingredients on package
- foil muffin liners
- food coloring
- bowls
- spoons
- straws

Directions

Prepare a white or yellow cake mix according to the instructions on the package. Pour a portion of batter into each of two small bowls. Add food coloring to these small bowls of batter. Gently spoon the original and colored batters in layers in the muffin tins. The top layer should be the original color of batter. Bake cupcakes as directed on the package.

When the cupcakes are cool, the real demonstration begins. Tell your child that the cupcake is like the Earth. Have her describe what she sees on the outside. Now, just as a geologist does, she is going to take a sampling of the "Earth" by putting her special tool (a straw) inside and gently pulling it out. (Putting the straw in at an angle makes this task easier.) Slit the straw to remove

the sampling. Now have her describe it. The activity will seem like magic, but explain that it is actually similar to what geologists do when they take core samplings to find out what is inside the earth's crust. Of course, geologists don't get to eat their samplings!

What Does Earth Look Like Inside?

This demonstration will help you explain how big, deep, and thick the world is.

Materials

- blue and brown tempera or acrylic paints
- an orange
- sharp knife (for adult use only)

Directions

With blue and brown paints, design some continents and oceans on the skin an orange. After the paint has dried, cut the orange in half. Show your child how the orange has many layers, just like the Earth. If you were to cut the Earth in half, it would look similar to this. The outer orange skin of the orange is like the crust of the Earth. It covers the whole earth and it is not very thick in comparison to the rest of the earth's insides. The next section the fruit is much thicker, like the next section of the Earth. But in the earth, it is very hot and liquidy. The very middle of the orange is like the core of the Earth. The Earth's core is solid and extremely hot. (The core of the Earth is actually broken up into the outer core and inner core.) Don't forget to explain that the deepest hole ever dug has not even gotten past the top layer of the earth.

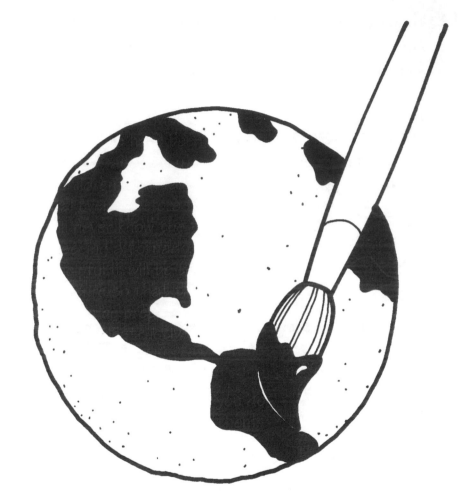

What Else?

Enjoy the book *How to Dig a Hole to the Other Side of the World* by Faith McNulty.

The Power of Nature

There are many things that are frightening to preschoolers: animal sounds in the night, flashing lightening in the sky, the wind howling, etc. Most of these things do not terrify adults because we have been around them long enough to know that they rarely do us any personal harm. We can do our children a big favor by helping them understand natural events before they happen. Hopefully, your child will never know the terror of being in a major earthquake or seeing a tornado, but the fact is many children do. How helpful it will be to them if they understand the power of nature so that they may not be so frightened. They also can be prepared if they do experience one of these powerful, destructive forces.

Where to Go

Of course, the thing with natural disasters is that you do not want to go to them, you want to go away from them. Keep your child as far as possible from any potential harmful event or element. Do not think that it will be a great adventure for your child to see a forest fire or a swirling tornado. Understand the potential physical danger. Psychological damage also can occur in children who are faced with disastrous events. Even television coverage and videos on natural disasters are not meant for preschoolers. If you want your child to see earthquake disaster footage or the power of a hurricane,

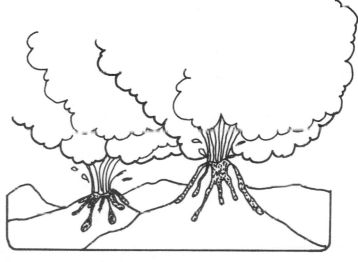

the best option is through books in the safety of your local library. The photographs chosen for books will not contain gruesome casualties that could frighten your child. The benefit of seeing pictures of these catastrophic events is to impress upon your preschooler the power of nature and the fact that we should never take nature or the weather for granted. All we can do is be prepared.

Natural history museums and children's science museums sometimes have exhibits, created especially for children, on earthquakes. Call a museum near you to see if they have any exhibits or special events that would be appropriate for a preschooler.

#2362 Exploring Nature

What to Do

A Pretend Quake

How does an earthquake work? Show your child this simple demonstration. You and your child stand facing each other and grab each others' wrists, keeping your arms straight. Stand perfectly still. Then one of you shake your arms in a jolt. The other person is to be passive, but this does not mean that his or her arms don't move. Now try this with a stuffed animal sitting on your arms. Try gentle and vigorous shakes. This is how a tremor from an earthquake spreads. A jolt happens under the ground, but that action causes a vibration that spreads until it's gone.

Put Together an Emergency Box

Your child can help you gather and collect these items, so you can be prepared in your car or home for any type of emergency.

- flashlight
- portable radio
- extra batteries
- first aid kit
- fire extinguisher
- clothing: 2 extra sets per person
- food: canned, dehydrated, powdered, stored in air-tight containers; enough for each person for at least three days
- water: 1 gallon per person per day for at least three days
- medication: at least one week's worth
- diapers and wipes (if you have a baby)

After you collect your important items, get out the paints and let your child decorate the supply box. You will need to use permanent paints, such as acrylics. Be sure to use work clothes on the painting day. Your child will enjoy brightening this container of important items, and the process will help make the experience fun rather than frightening. (**Note:** Change the batteries, food items, and water every six months or so to ensure fresh supplies if you ever need to use them.)

Make a Tornado Bottle

This is an easy-to-make science experiment that will entertain your child.

Materials

- two 2-liter soda bottles
- water
- food coloring (optional)
- electrical tape

Directions

Fill one of the bottles about ²/₃ with water and add the food coloring just for fun. Match the other bottle to the first by turning it upside down and putting the mouths of the bottles together. Use the electrical tape to attach the two bottles, being sure that they are secure. Turn the first bottle upside down, and while swishing the top bottle in a circular motion, hold the bottom bottle steady. Watch the tornado of water that moves into the second bottle. (**Note:** It is best to do this activity outside or in the bathtub where a leak will not be a problem.)

What Else?

Read *Come a Tide* by George-Ella Lyon.

Show the Power Inside a Volcano

For children who aren't afraid of loud noises, here's an activity you can do together.

Materials

- balloon
- bicycle pump

Directions

Attach a balloon to the end of a bicycle pump. Hold onto the balloon as you pump, watching the pressure inside the balloon build up. Soon the balloon will not be able to hold any more pressure, and the balloon will explode. This simulates the pressure inside the Earth that builds up until it releases in the form of a volcanic eruption.

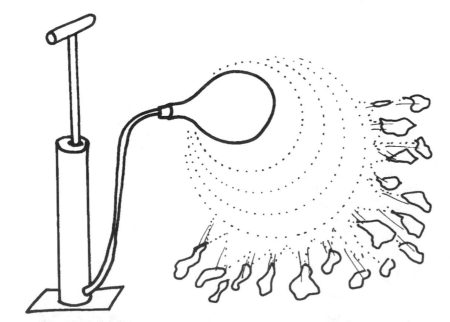

Make a Volcano

Hopefully, this will be the closest you will ever get to a live volcanic eruption.

Materials

- sand
- baking soda
- foil
- red food coloring
- spray bottle of water
- vinegar
- liquid soap

Directions

Wet the sand and mound it to create a mountain shape. With your fingers, push into the top to make a deep indentation. Make a tube shape with foil that will fit into the hole in the sand mountain. Into the tube, mix a couple of teaspoons of baking soda with a tablespoon of water, two drops of liquid soap, and two drops of red food coloring. Gently place the foil tube into the mountain (Don't get any sand in it!) and press the sand around it. Add a teaspoon of vinegar and watch pretend lava pour out of the volcano. Your child will want to do this again and again. You can repeat the results by shaking in a little more baking soda and then a few drops of vinegar.

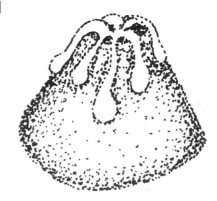

92

Water

Walking Along the Ocean

Salt, sand, surf—adults and children alike enjoy the atmosphere that is unique to the seaside. At least once in your life, try to take a barefoot walk on the beach; even better, watch your child enjoy one. The sights and smells of the ocean have a freeing effect on children as they chase the sea gulls over stretches of sand and watch waves crash on the beach.

But the ocean is more than sand and sea salt. It is an ecosystem, a habitat for many species from sand crabs to sharks. As you show your preschooler the many forms of life on the beach and in the ocean, you will notice many differences in this habitat from the ones you usually enjoy.

Most people do not live near an ocean. If you do not have the opportunity to enjoy an authentic beach experience, hopefully you can enjoy a quality nature center in your area that has ocean exhibits. The Internet also has sites related to the ocean (page 157). None of this, of course, is as impressive as an actual experience, but it is still interesting to learn about this large part of our world.

Whether experiencing the ocean is new for your preschooler or something you do every summer, you will be able to enjoy it from a fresh perspective with some of the activities on the next few pages.

Salt Water

"Water, water everywhere/Nor any drop to drink" are famous lines from Samuel Taylor Coleridge's "Rime of the Ancient Mariner." It's a funny thought to a child: an ocean filled with water that cannot be used to quench thirst. More than 70% of the Earth's surface is covered with water, and most of that is salty. Salt water might not be good for us to drink, but it makes a perfect home for the sea life that lives there.

As you look at the ocean with your child, ask questions like how far out can you see? What do you think happens when you sail to the horizon? Why do you feel clean after a bath at home but sticky after a dip in the ocean?

Where to Go

The best place to enjoy salt water is, of course, at the ocean or a salt water river. For the activities below, you can make your own salt water, but it will not sustain sea life. The best thing about the ocean is that it can be perceived with all of the five senses. Many beaches have areas where the tide goes out, leaving pools of water in the rocks called "tide pools." Tide pools are perhaps the most personal experience you can have with the sea life. Be sure to take a magnifying glass to really let your child inspect the homes of anemones, barnacles, and tiny fish. But don't take anything away from these habitats.

Aquariums have salt water exhibits that include plants and animals. This is a wonderful opportunity for children to see animals in their natural habitat.

What to Do

Experiencing the Ocean through the Senses

We have five senses, and all of them can be used to experience the ocean. Tell your child you are going to use your body to understand the ocean in five different ways. First you are going to hear it. Don't engage any other part of your body but your ears. What does the ocean sound like? Make imitative sounds. Next, use your eyes to see what it looks like and then your nose to smell the sea water. Now have your child, under your supervision, stand at the edge of the surf to feel the water. Last,

have a little taste! Just a few drops on the tongue will get the point across that this is different water than what you drink at home. Review the ways your body experienced the ocean: hearing, seeing, smelling, feeling, tasting. Can you use them all at once?

What Else?

How many things at the ocean begin with the sound made by the letter S? Here are a few: sand, sea, salt, seashell, sand dollar. Can you think of more? Make giant S's in the sand.

Try Some Floating Experiments

Lots of things float in water, even more so when the water contains salt. Choose a few items from your purse or the beach and test whether or not they float. Here are some things to try: a feather, a Styrofoam cup, a coin, a small piece of paper, a crayon, a small piece of driftwood, a pencil. Be sure to pick up your trash and put it in a trash can when you are finished.

Float a Boat of Pennies

After you've experimented with floating, try this more advanced game.

Materials

- pennies
- plastic container
- washtub or pail

Directions

Use a lightweight, empty, plastic container, such as one that once contained yogurt. Place the container in a washtub or pail filled with water. Have your child guess how many pennies she can put in the container before it starts to sink. One? Five? Ten? This is a great counting game, as well as good practice in estimating. Try it in salt water and fresh water. Is there any difference in the number of pennies you can add before the container sinks?

Making Salt

What else is in the ocean besides water? Find out with this parent-demonstrated activity.

Materials

- ocean water or homemade salt water (1 part salt to 2 parts water)
- saucepan

Directions

Place salt water in the saucepan and put the heat on low. Set the timer for 30 minutes to see what happens. You may need to check back with your experiment a couple of times, but eventually you will notice that once the water has evaporated, salt rings appear around the saucepan. After the pan is cooled, have your child taste the salt.

Caution: Only an adult should handle the heat controls, stove top, or any of the materials for this experiment. To prevent ruining your pot or causing a fire, watch your pot carefully once you notice the water level reducing.

What Else?

Before or after a trip to the sea, read Charlotte Zolotow's *The Seashore Book.*

Making Waves

This easy-to-make wave machine will mesmerize your little one.

Materials

- 2-liter soda bottle
- sand
- water
- blue or green food coloring
- electrical tape (optional)

Directions

Clean out the bottle. Fill it with about a cup of sand, and then add water until the bottle is about half full. Add a few drops of blue and green food coloring until you are pleased with the look of your ocean water. Cap the bottle tightly, sealing it with electrical tape if you'd like. Put a hole in the side of the bottle. Gently shake the bottle back and forth to watch it make waves. Watch the sand settle, just like it does in the ocean.

What Else?

How fast can you say the tongue twister "She sells seashells by the seashore?"

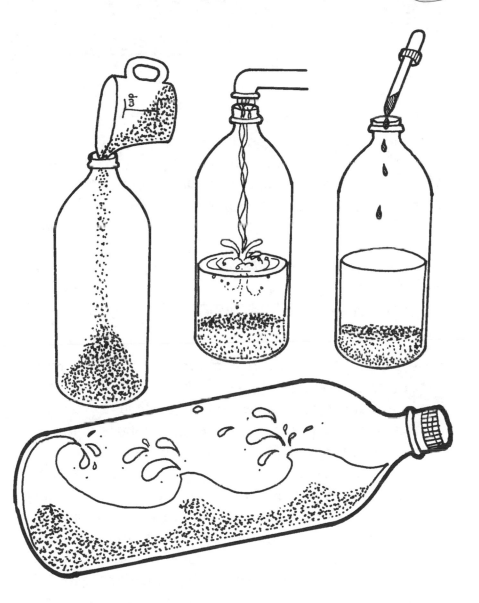

Fish and Sea Animals

When you look out at the ocean, it is hard to believe that another world exists below the surface. Everything from the world's largest living creature to some of the smallest forms of life make up the underwater ecosystem. Salt water fish, sea mammals, plants, and shells are part of this beautiful world. A real underwater visit may not be possible. Fortunately there are many ways to become acquainted with ocean life such as books and videos. Depending on where you live, you may see some exciting animals in or near the ocean. Watch for whales, dolphins, otters, and a variety of fish, which you will be able to see if the water is clear.

Shells are an important part of sea life. They are home to many small animals. There are two types of shells, univalves and bivalves. Univalves are a singular shell, often with a spiral. Some examples are conch shells and smooth, spotted cowries. Bivalves come in pairs, although you usually see only half their shells at a time. These are the ones you can picture opening up on a hinge. Some examples are mussel shells, scallops, and clam shells. Either type will be a delight to children. You are likely to see some on any beach, especially if you dig a little, but your luck will improve if you take a strainer with you for a shell hunt. After a storm, when things have been tossed and turned more than usual under the surface, you may find a great assortment of shells.

Anything organic that you remove from the ocean must be returned (as it may be needed as an animal home). You will be able to enjoy that moment of excitement when your child sees something in a way he or she has never seen it before.

Where to Go

A great place to see sea life is in tide pools. You may be able to see small fish, sea anenomes, sea urchins, sand dollars, barnacles, muscle shells, and a variety of tiny fish. Be sure to take a magnifying glass to let your child closely inspect this animal habitat. It is extremely important to leave a tide pool just as you found it. This is a natural opportunity to explain that our actions have consequences on these delicate animals.

Aquariums have salt water exhibits that include plants and animals. This is a wonderful opportunity for children to see animals in their natural habitat.

Finally, a field trip to an exotic fish store can be very educational if you can arrange to go during the week, when the store is quiet and personnel are available to answer questions.

What to Do

Have Crab Races

It's hard work being a crab, which you will discover when you have your own crab race.

After you have looked at pictures of crabs, show your child how you can look like a crab, too. Sit on your bottom with your hands reaching behind you. Push yourself up, so that you are resting on your hands and feet. Now try to move forward and backward. After a little bit of practice, you will be ready for a family crab race.

Listen to a Shell

Adults know that they will hear a hissing sound like the sea when they hold a shell to the ear, but it might be interesting to find out what your child says she hears. Hold a univalve shell to your ear. The bigger, the better! What sound does it make? Before you coach your child by saying, "It sounds like the ocean, doesn't it?" give her some time to really listen. She will probably come up with some very different answers than what you might expect.

What Else?

Read Marcus Pfister's story about giving, *Rainbow Fish*. *Swimmy*, by Leo Lionni, is a sponge-painted underwater tale your child will love, too.

Sort Sea Shells

Sorting and classifying is fun, especially if it looks like an ocean-related game.

Help your child sort shells many different ways: rough and smooth; whole shells and broken shells; single-colored and multi-colored; univalve and bivalve. Continue to add to the seashell collection and sort the shells a new way each time. See page 152 for ways to store collections.

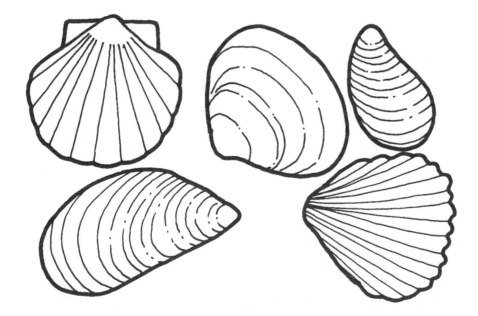

Tuna in a Cone

Try this traditional seafood recipe served in a unique way.

Ingredients

- 6.5 oz. can of tuna
- $1/3$ c. mayonnaise
- 2 tablespoons sweet pickle relish
- ice cream cones

Directions

Mix together the first three ingredients, scoop them into a cone, and top with a cherry tomato or an olive.

What Else?

See what it feels like to be an otter. Read Sea Elf by Joanne Ryder.

Water Jars

You may not be able to take live ocean creatures home with you, but you can make models.

Materials

- white Styrofoam meat trays
- colored permanent markers
- brightly-colored cellophane
- scissors
- baby food jars
- clear packing tape

Directions

Draw small fish, starfish, and other ocean animals on the foam packaging. Cut them out. Cut out the cellophane in shapes of ocean plants like seaweed. Put the items in the baby food jar and fill with water. Cap the jar and seal with packing tape. Shake to see the animals "swim."

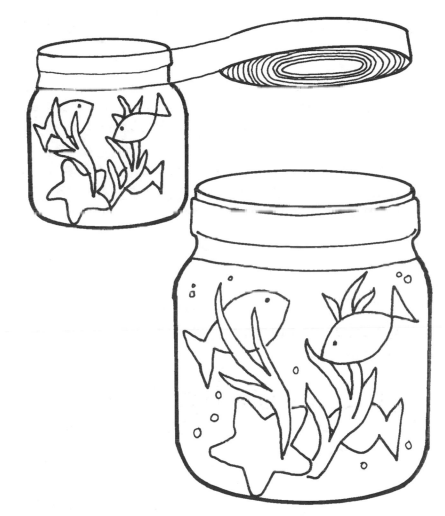

What Else?

Read Brian Wildsmith's *Fishes* for one author's colorful view of the sea.

Sandy Shores

Sand is associated with beaches—oceans, lakes, creeks, and shores of all kinds. Sand helps to define where the land ends and the water begins. The best thing about sand is also the worst thing about sand—it's gritty. Sand has a unique texture that feels warm and soft between your fingers, but annoying when it gets under nails and into bathing suits.

The best way to remove sand from your child's body is with baby powder. Be sure the child is completely dry and you have brushed off what you can. Then sprinkle and pat the powder on the skin. Most of the sand will flake off. The powder absorbs moisture so that the sand no longer sticks to the skin.

Where to Go

Of course, the best place to enjoy sand is at the beach. It's fun to try different beaches because the sand often differs form beach to beach. At some beaches the sand is extremely fine and white, at some it is coarse, and at some you will find the ground quite rocky with almost no sand at all.

If you don't live near a body of water that has good, clean sand, you can still do the projects on the next pages with the help of your local hardware or home improvement store. They carry bags full of sand that is perfect for sandboxes and sand crafts.

Sand Play

Keeping it simple is sometimes the most fun.

Grab a bunch of kitchen items that you don't mind getting a little gritty and take them with you on your sand adventure. A big kitchen colander used for straining pasta is much more appealing to a preschooler than the little one that comes with sand toy kits. Also bring along big spoons, spatulas, and plastic bowls and lids. Vary the sizes and colors. If the sand is dry, keep a plastic pitcher or watering can full of water for different sand and water experiences.

Build Sand Cities

Sand castles are just the beginning when you play in the sand. With the items previously mentioned, plus empty juice and yogurt containers, you can build an entire city of sand structures. Use as many different sizes as you can to add variety to your city. The key to sand castles and other buildings is the consistency of the sand, which must be wet but not goopy. Experiment until you and your child find the perfect amount of moisture for your city. Make a plan and mark off the amount of space you want to fill with buildings. Start by making a ditch or moat by the side closest to the waves. A spray bottle filled with colored water will help to keep the sand buildings moist and stable, as well as add a decorative touch. Also, decorate with shells, seaweed, bottle caps, and other objects found in the sand.

Create a Beach Collage

Take the beach experience and its special memories home with you.

Materials

- various items found at the beach
- clean Styrofoam meat tray
- white glue
- sand

Directions

As you stroll along the beach with your preschooler, you will find many fun items that you can't find anywhere else. Help your child collect broken shells, stones, driftwood, seaweed, and anything else that will remind her of the beach, as well as a scoop of sand saved in a plastic bag. Double check the shells to make sure they are really empty or you may have an unexpected "guest" when you get them. When you get home, arrange the items on a clean Styrofoam meat tray. Remove them, then smear some white glue on the bottom half of the tray and sprinkle on the sand. After it dries, glue on the other items you collected in the arrangement you desire, and you will have a beautiful reminder of your day in the sand.

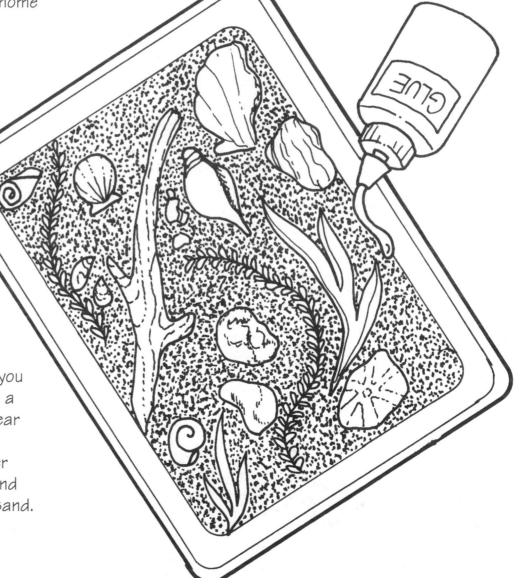

106

Make Your Own Sand

Sand at the beach has been pounded by waves crashing up against the rocky shore, but you can create your own sand. This is an activity that should be done by an adult and observed by the younger set.

Materials

- small rocks
- old pillowcase
- hammer
- fine mesh colander

Directions

Collect some small rocks and put them in a pillow case. (The pillowcase must be one you don't need to use again, as it will get torn.) With a hammer, pound the rocks vigorously. When your child decides it is time, open the pillowcase and pour the rock mixture through a colander. What comes out will be fine sand!

Play in a Sand Tray

Used as favorite developmental activity by preschool teachers, a sand tray will just seem like a lot of fun to your little one.

Materials

- jelly roll pan
- sand
- items for making imprints

Directions

Pour about a cup of sand onto the cookie sheet. Show your child how to make swirls and lines and even how to practice his or her name. Add items that will make imprints in the sand, like small blocks or clean yogurt containers. This is a great outdoor or kitchen table activity. For easy cleanup, just pour the sand into a resealable plastic bag and save for the next sand-tray adventure.

Make Colored Sand Pictures

You don't need a fancy kit to make pretty pictures with colored sand.

Materials

- clean sand
- liquid food coloring
- sandwich-size, resealable plastic bags
- construction paper or cardboard
- white glue or glue stick

Directions

Put up to a ½ cup of sand in each bag with two or three drops of liquid food coloring. Seal and shake. Open the bags to allow sand to dry overnight. Make a glue design. Pour on the desired color of sand. Let it set before adding more glue and another color of sand. Continue until your design is complete. (**Note:** For preschoolers, it is easier to create a design than a full picture. Let their creativity be the guide.)

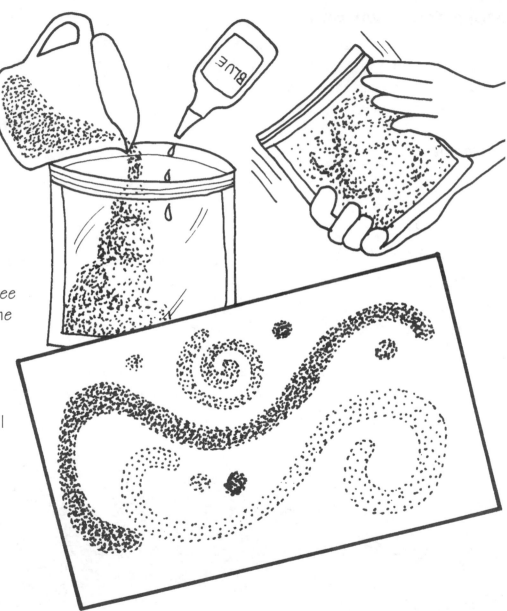

Make Homemade Sandpaper

Teach your child that sand can be a valuable tool.

Materials

- 2" x 2" block of wood
- construction paper
- two small nails
- white glue
- sand

Directions

Coat a section of the paper with glue and sprinkle sand on top. Pat it down, then shake off the excess. It may take a day for the sandpaper to completely dry. Fold it over the wooden block and nail the paper in place. Compare this homemade sandpaper to what you may already have on hand. Will the homemade version work the same as store bought? Give it a try and see.

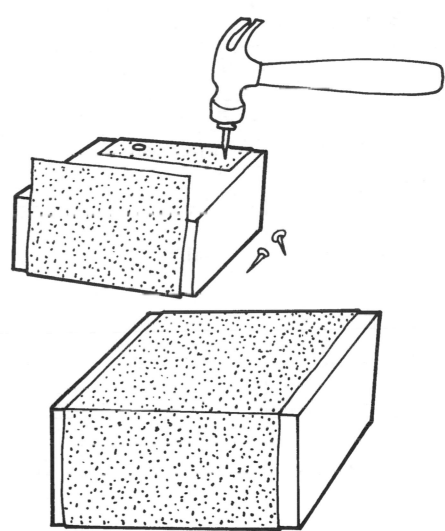

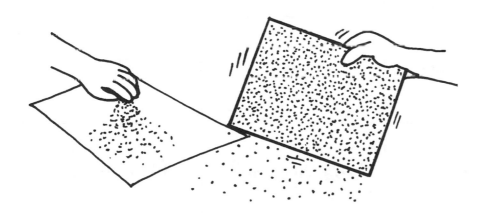

What Else?

The nonfiction book *Talk About Sand* by Angela Webb is an excellent resource.

Play Beach Bingo

Who is best able to find certain items in the sand or in the water? Make a copy of this page to take to the beach. Use small stones, shell pieces, or a pencil to mark off the square, and see who can get five in a row.

bottle cap	starfish	cone-shaped shell	sand	sunblock
sand crab	sailboat	dog	plastic straw	leaf
soda can	sea gull	**FREE**	plastic beach toys	sea anemone
bathing suit	sand dollar	beach towel	seaweed	fish
small rock	broken shell	driftwood	scallop shell	bird tracks

Walking Along Fresh Water

Water is not just plain liquid. It is a home for many different types of life. Without water, there would be no life at all on Earth. You may live near a lake, river, pond, stream, or brook. However, if none of those are within walking distance, you can make your own puddles. No matter what type of fresh water you have near you, there is a habitat of plant and animal life in that area, as well. Your preschooler will enjoy exploring with you as you find tadpoles and pussy willows by the pond, smooth stones that have had water rolling over them for years in a river or stream, and schools of fish varieties in your local lake.

With your magnifying glass in hand, seek and study the beauty of fresh water habitats by using the activities on the next few pages.

As you prepare for a trip to the lake or river, remember to pack waterproof sunblock and insect repellent. Also be prepared for wet and muddy shores; rain boots work well for lake walks.

Enjoy the miniature world of plant and animal life contained in a water garden. Ponds, lakes, and rivers have much excitement to offer a child.

Pond Life

Sea water is a perfect home for a whale—but not a frog! It might all be water, but the habitat and experiences are completely different. Where the ocean is an expansive home, a pond or lake is usually more quiet and contained, with inhabitants that are more reliant on the surrounding land. Of course, another obvious difference is that fresh water is salt-free. It comes from rain and melted snowfall, often traveling many miles through mountain passes to become part of a larger expanse of water, sometimes even reaching an ocean.

Life in a pond is an incredible microcosm. Mammals, reptiles, and insects all feed from the pond's water and the plants that grow around it. There are also unique sounds in this special environment—crickets, birds, frogs, and owls are just some of the noisemakers that make the pond or lake their home. Also, with all of the interesting plants, a pond is a beautiful water garden.

If the pond is a new experience for your child, have him compare it to the ocean. How are these two water homes the same and different? What kinds of animals live in each? Where would he rather live—in a wide ocean, a crashing waterfall, or a peaceful pond?

Where to Go

You probably can find a body of fresh water near your home. To find animals that live in or near fresh water, look in ponds, streams, lakes, and rivers. If you have access to both fresh and salt water environments, take a sampling of both types of water in similar jars. Compare the color, smell, and stuff floating around in it. When you visit a pond or lake, be sure to take a net with fine mesh, a magnifying glass, a waterscope (instructions on page 113), and a couple of jars for holding any creature you want to inspect.

Pet stores often display and sell animals that enjoy fresh water homes: frogs, toads, snakes, and fish. The animal keepers will be able to help you understand these animals' environments and the foods they eat. You may also want to find out the feeding schedule so you can watch this event.

What to Do

Skipping Stones

Skipping stones is one of those childhood memories that everyone should have. If you are right-handed, hold your right arm out to your side, palm side up and bent a little at the elbow. Hold your hand like you are going to open a very small door knob. Hold a smooth, flat stone between your thumb and index finger. Cock your wrist back and swing your arm forward, releasing the stone. Remember, it takes practice! The key is to keep the stone parallel to the water. After some practice, you will long remember the day when your little one skips one in. But if your child wants to toss stones in just to see the mesmerizing rings, so be it.

Make a Waterscope

Better than television—it's watervision!

Materials

- cylindrical cardboard or plastic ice cream container
- craft knife (for adult use only)
- plastic wrap
- large rubber bands

Directions

Cut the bottom from the ice cream container. Cut off a piece of plastic wrap that fits over the hole with four or more inches to spare. Put the plastic wrap on a table, place the ice cream container on top, and smooth the plastic wrap up over the edges. Hold the plastic wrap in place with one or two large rubber bands. This nifty scope can be used directly in the water.

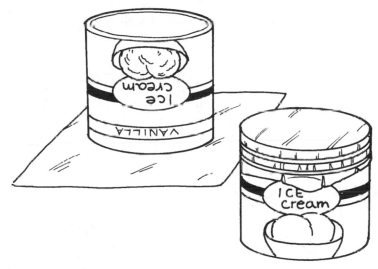

What Else?

Enjoy the stunning photographs in Mark Rauson's *Water, Water Everywhere.*

 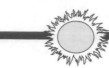

Play a Game of Leap Frog

Don't forget to say "Ribbit!" as you play this simple childhood game.

It will be easier for you to play the frog and to hop over your child than for her to hop over you, but it's good to try it both ways. Have your little one crouch down on the ground, tucking in arms, legs, and head. Gently press your hands on her back and hop over. Then crouch down and she can do the same to you, except that you can expect to be sat on. Ribbit!

Be a Water Strider

Water bugs love pond life. Water striders live and move on top of the surface of the water. After you have polished your floor, have your little one put on two pairs of socks, one on his feet and one on his hands. Assume the water bug position by putting hands and feet on the floor, and bend and glide those legs as a water strider would.

Weave Reeds

Native Americans used reeds and tall grasses to make mats, but you can encourage your child to use natural materials from the pond area to practice the fine art of weaving.

Find about 10 reeds or long pieces of straight grass that are similar in length. Lay five of them flat next to each other. Begin weaving with the next one by putting over one reed, under the next, continuing through all five reeds. The next reed gets woven under, then over. Continue in this manner, tightening the weave as you go. If your child perseveres, she will make a nice woven mat to sit on while at the pond.

Wish for a Fish

You don't need a fancy fishing rod to be a full-fledged fisherman. For your child to be successful at fishing, you will need a sturdy stick about a yard long. Tie some fishing line to one end. If you want to use a hook, you can, but your child may be just as happy to tie on a worm or a piece of cheese and toss the line in the water. An alternative way for younger children is to toss some fine bread crumbs into the water and scoop up into the net any fish that bite.

Make an Aquarium

After seeing frogs, ducks, and fish at a pond, your child may want his own pond friends.

You can find various-sized aquariums at pet shops and discount stores. Add sand or aquarium gravel, a few rocks of assorted sizes, a branch, and small plants. Fill the aquarium about half full of water, being sure to leave part of the rock and stick uncovered. After the water clears, add a frog or turtle to this aquarium home. For best results, get a book from your library on setting up aquariums. Unless you're prepared to keep your aquarium clean, (and this means cleaning twice a week) this might not be the hobby for you.

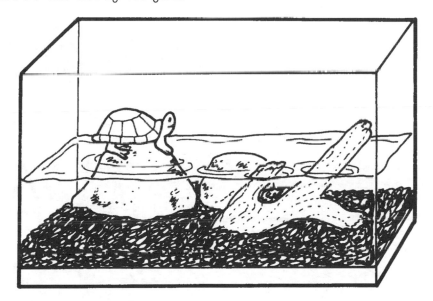

What Else?

Where the River Begins is a beautifully illustrated story by Thomas Locker about a special hike two children take with their grandfather.

See How Fish Breathe

Instead of lungs, fish have gills. You can actually watch the gills work with this colorful demonstration.

Using an eyedropper, fill it with some colored water (3 drops of food coloring to 1/2 cup of water). Put the dropper into the water and release the colored water as close to the fish's mouth as possible. Watch as the fish inhales the colored water and expels it out of his gills.

Play Big Fish, Little Fish

You can pretend to be a fish in a pond, lake, or swimming pool. If you are playing in a lake or pond, set some boundaries for the area in which the game will be played. The parent is the "big fish" and waits in the middle of the water with eyes closed. When he says, "I'm hungry, little fish," the child moves from one end of the water to the other. The big fish tries to capture the little fish, while still keeping his eyes closed.

What Else?

Read about a little girl's adventure with a frog in *Tale of a Tadpole* by Barbara Ann Porte.

116

Sky

117

Walking with Weather

The mail carrier's creed tells us that the mail must be delivered, no matter what the weather conditions. Since life has to go on despite weather conditions, there's no reason we can't try to enjoy each day's weather as it comes.

It is fortunate that you can go anywhere on Earth and see the sun during many days of the year. You can enjoy a sunny walk on a beach, in an orchard, in a forest, or just in your neighborhood. But walks are not limited to warm, sunny days. Delight in spending time with your child in a variety of weather conditions. As long as you are dressed appropriately, a walk with the weather is an adventure.

The elements of heat, air, and water work together to create different types and varying degrees of weather. The nice thing about weather is that you don't have to go anywhere to find it. Almost anywhere in the world will have a variety of weather conditions to experience in even a month's time. Don't let the weather be only the backdrop for your involvement in nature. Learn to make it part of your nature walk equation. The activities on the next few pages lend themselves to all types of weather. After you experience or read about different types of weather, try some of the activities to help your child learn about how weather is formed and affects us.

Weather Calendar

Copy and cut out the chart and symbols. Each day your child can decide which symbol best represents the weather. Color the symbol and glue it to the chart. When it is complete, count the number of symbols on the chart. Compare how many more days of one type of weather you experienced than another.

Sunday	Monday	Tuesday	Wednesday	Thursday	Friday	Saturday

Cloudy Rainy Sunny Snowy Partly Cloudy

Cloudy Rainy Sunny Snowy Partly Cloudy

#2362 Exploring Nature

Temperature

Hot, cold, warm, freezing, balmy, humid—there are so many words to describe the temperature. Even with the variety we enjoy, we are fortunate that the temperature span on our Earth is only about 100° F/38° C. What temperatures do you enjoy the most? The heat of summer? The brisk, cold wind of winter? There are advantages to each, and your child can probably tell them to you. Have a look at the chart below to compare temperatures that are important in our lives.

Temperature	Fahrenheit	Celsius
freezing	32°	0°
comfortable	75°	23.9°
average baking temperature	350°	173.3°
temperature at which paper burns	450°	272.2°

Encourage your child to estimate the temperature and enjoy the spectrum we have in daily temperatures.

Where to Go

Although a book on nature activities might rarely persuade you to turn on the television, one of the best ways to encourage your child to understand weather and daily temperature is to watch the meteorologist on your local TV news. With wonderful, colorful graphics and large numbers, the weather person shows the daily temperatures in your area. Take time to talk about what types of activities might be limited because of the weather.

What to Do

Make a Thermometer

This thermometer uses kid power, not mercury, to show the temperature. Children need to learn the mechanics of thermometers. Show your little one that when the red line goes up, it means it is hot; when the red line goes down, it means it is cooler. Can you trick him?

Materials

- white construction paper
- red construction paper
- black marker
- scissors

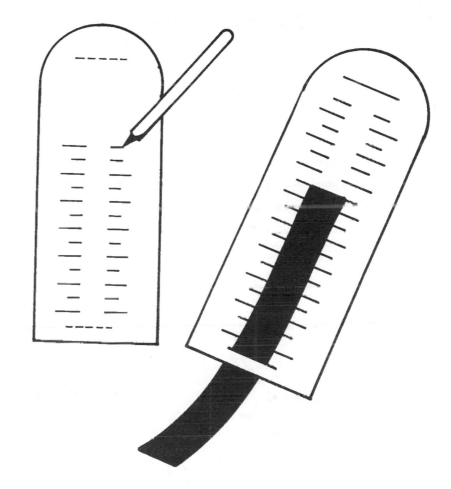

Directions

Cut a thermometer shape out of white construction paper. Label the sides with horizontal temperature markings. Break up your degree markings by five degrees, but don't be too concerned about the numbers—knowing that up is hot and down is cold is more important than the numbers at this age. Slit the top and bottom of the thermometer. Cut a thin piece of red construction paper that can slide easily through the slits. Demonstrate the up and down movement of the red line.

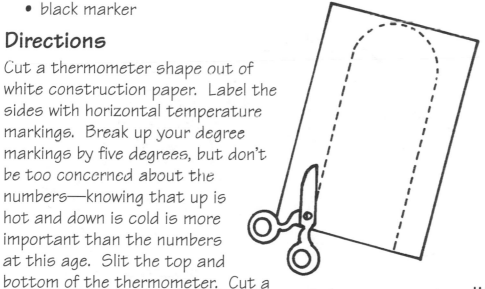

What Else?

The hottest temperature ever recorded was in Al Aziziyah, Libya, where it was 136° F/58° C on September 13, 1922.

Dress Teddy for the Weather

No matter what the temperature outside, you can test your little one's weather skills by having her dress Teddy for a variety of weather situations.

Materials

- large stuffed bear
- clothes representing various weather conditions (examples: snow cap, bathing suit, boots, mittens, sunglasses, sweater, sandals)

Directions

Lay out a variety of seasonal clothing in no particular order. With a "Ready, set, go!" have your child dress Teddy for a hot day at the beach, a cold day in the snow, or a cool, windy day. How long will it take him to change Teddy to match a new weather situation?

What Else?

How Do You Say It Today, Jesse Bear? by Nancy White Carlstrom is a delightful rhyming story showing preschool hero Jesse Bear dressing for every month of the year.

Sunny Days Are Here Again

Virtually everyone likes the sun, as long as it's not too warm. It is amazing that the largest energy source in our solar system provides so much energy. You can surprise your child with facts such as these:

- ☼ The sun is really a star.
- ☼ Our planet, the Earth, moves around the sun.
- ☼ Plants and animals could not grow without the sun.

It will take time for your child to grasp these concepts, so you should expect to repeat them many times.

The swirling ball of gases we call our sun, a relatively small and young star, has a couple of important jobs to do, including providing energy through heat and evaporating water to rejoin the water cycle. Without the sun, our planet could not exist because we would have no source of energy. The gravity of our sun also keeps us from being pulled into some other system that has a planet or star with a stronger gravitational pull. In some ways, you might say the sun is the most important thing in the solar system.

But on a hot day, none of that matters. Enjoy the sun on those days as a tool for proving evaporation and energy, as explained in the fun projects that follow.

Where to Go

If you live near a beach or a desert, it would be worth your time to visit one during a sunset. You can often enjoy the beauty of a sunset in these settings because the clouds cover the sun during much of the process. Do warn your children, however, of the danger of looking directly into the sun.

Wide-open spaces like deserts and beaches provide idyllic views for the majesty of color changes. Have your child enjoy the cloud colors for a few moments, and then have him close his eyes and imagine what the sunset will look like next. When he opens his eyes, is he right?

Because you will enjoy the sun on many of your walks, remember to be prepared with sunblock.

What to Do

Play Shadow Tag

Enjoy this variation of regular tag on a bright, sunny day.

This is a less aggressive game than traditional tag, as there is no direct contact. It's best to play around 10:00 a.m. or after 2:00 p.m., when shadows are long. You can be "it" and try to tag your child, which you do by stepping on the shadow of the other players. Running and ducking are the primary modes of play. After you tag your child's shadow, let him or her be "it." This game is almost guaranteed to get everyone laughing.

Have a Melting Contest

This activity will keep you so cool on a hot day that you may want to repeat it several times. Each player should have an ice cube. The object is to see who can melt his ice cube the fastest without putting it in his mouth. You might get a little wet, but you'll be a whole lot more comfortable in the heat.

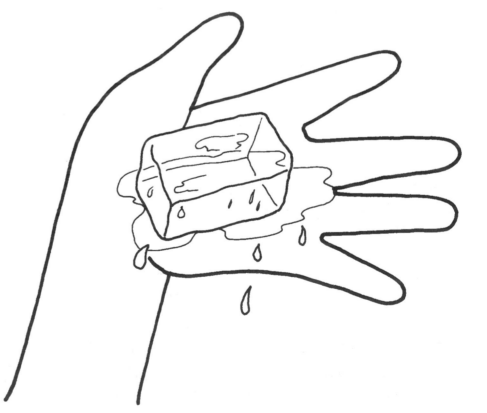

124

Make Sun X-Rays

You won't need any high-tech equipment to produce x-rays made by the sun.

Materials

- dark construction paper
- objects with distinct shapes (e.g., hammer, book, shoe)
- sunny location

Directions

Place a few objects on the construction paper in direct sunlight for a few hours. The exposed paper will slowly discolor, but where you placed your items the color will remain strong. You can introduce the word "fade," and the concept of the sun's power will become real to your child as she holds her faded picture in hand.

Do an Evaporation Demonstration

On black or dark construction paper, have your child draw a picture with an ice cube. Once completed, leave the picture in the sun for awhile. When you come back, the picture will have disappeared. This would be a great time to talk about the power of the sun and how it made the water evaporate.

Make a Simple Sundial

This sundial will be a great demonstration of how people long ago told time before clocks were invented.

Materials

- paper plate
- scissors
- tape

Directions

Cut the plate in half. One half will be the base. With the remaining piece, cut a triangle (called a *gnomon*) that will cover the radius of the base. Fold down about an inch of the triangle and tape it to the base. Put the sun dial in the sun (with the gnomon pointing north) and watch the sun cast its moving shadow.

What Else?

How many words can you think of that rhyme with *sun*? Can you make a tongue twister with words that start with the *S* sound?

Rain, Rain, Go Away

As a child you sang:

> Rain, rain, go away
>
> Come again another day.

But there is no reason to send rain away, because rain is fun! It is also fascinating to preschoolers that water falls from the sky. The mystery of clouds filling with water and then losing it in drops causes children to ask all sorts of questions about rain.

A rainy day gives you a wonderful opportunity to introduce the concept of the rain cycle. During a rain walk or view from your window, ask your child questions about rain, such as, Where does the rain come from? How much water do you think is falling right now? If it is raining here, is it raining at Grandma's house? (Give Grandma a call and have your child ask.)

Where to Go

The best thing about rain is that you don't have to go anywhere to find it. If you wait long enough, it will come to you. Enjoying nature in the rain is completely different than a dry nature walk. Put on your rain boots and some old jeans, prepare the towels, then go out and smell and feel the wet world around you.

#2362 Exploring Nature

What to Do

Create a Chalk Drawing

This is a fun activity for a day when light rain is predicted. If your child has seen the movie "Mary Poppins," remind him or her of the scene in which Bert makes chalk drawings on the sidewalk. When rain is imminent, become sidewalk artists and make chalk drawings on your driveway or sidewalk, just like Bert did. Be sure to fill in the picture heavily with the colored chalk. As it starts to rain, the edges will become faded and the colors will run together, making a pretty design. Be sure your child is aware that the drawing will not only get wet but will be changed in the water.

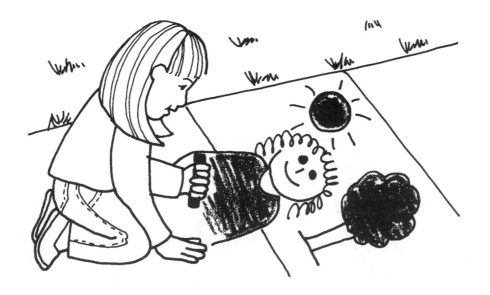

Have a Puddle Dance

If it is too wet to play in the rain outside, create some puddles in your own living room. Cut several puddle shapes from blue construction paper and lightly tape them to your floor. Call out commands to your child to move from puddle to puddle such as hop, jump, and go backwards. For extra fun, have your child don his rain gear during this activity.

Recreate the Sound of Rain

This musical, rhythmic game really mimics the sounds of a rain storm. The more people to play this game with you, the more realistic it sounds, but it still works and is lots of fun for only two people. Have your child follow your hand movements as you use them to make rain sounds. With your child sitting across from you on the floor, start by slowly rubbing your hands together, and then slowly start snapping your fingers together. (If this skill is too difficult for your child, have her gently slap her cheeks.) Then slowly start slapping your legs with your hands. Make a couple of foot stomps while your are rubbing for the sound of thunder. After slapping your legs wildly for awhile, start slowing down and reversing the rain-making process.

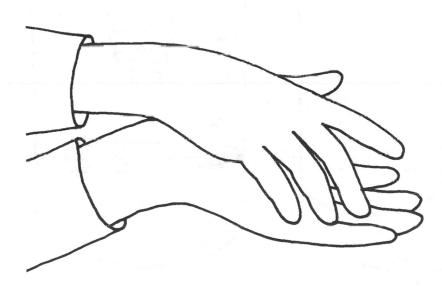

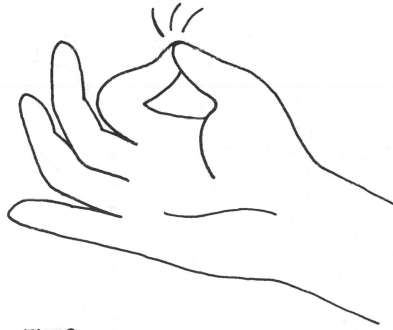

What Else?

Robert Kallan's *Rain* is the perfect preschool rain book.

Make a Rain Gauge

Although not perfectly scientific, this homemade tool will help your child learn how measurements are taken.

Materials

- 2-liter plastic soda bottle
- craft knife or scissors (for adult use only)
- permanent marker
- ruler

Directions

Wash and dry a plastic soda bottle. Cut away the top third of the bottle. Invert the top section to use as a funnel, setting it on the bottom section of the bottle. If rain is coming down hard, you might want to reinforce this tool with two-sided tape between the two pieces. Starting 2" from the bottom of the bottle, use the permanent marker to mark off inches up the side of the bottle. Add water to the first line. Set your instrument out in the rain and await the official results.

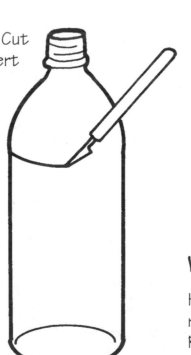

What Else?

How many nursery rhymes can you think of that mention rain? Start with "It's Raining, It's Pouring," and "Rain, Rain, Go Away."

All the Colors of the Rainbow

Is there anything more beautiful than a rainbow? A rainbow hangs like a colored arc in the sky, a treat after a dreary, rainy day. But there is solid science behind every band of color in the sky. A rainbow is the reflection of the sun's rays in individual drops of water—a rainbow always appears directly opposite the sun. The arc of a rainbow is a full circle, but you can only see this from the air. Sometimes the light reflects twice, making a rare double rainbow. The colors of a rainbow always go in this order: red, orange, yellow, green, blue, indigo, violet.

Most of the questions you ask your child about rainbows will center on color. Try these:

- Can you name the colors in the rainbow?
- What colors do you not see?
- What colors would you put in a rainbow?

Then, of course, there are fanciful questions which are appropriate to the whimsical appearance of a rainbow.

- How would you ride down a rainbow?
- What is at the end of the rainbow?
- Why do you think there are rainbows?

Where to Go

Of course, there is no one special place you can go to visit rainbows, but the next time you see one after a storm, how about attempting a journey to its end? This nature drive in your car will be most fun if your preschooler gets to be the ultimate backseat driver, calling directions to reach the rainbow. Make sure that your futile journey ends happily at your local ice cream store for some rainbow sherbet.

Children's or science museums often have exhibits about light, prisms, and/or rainbows. Call ahead to see if your local museum has an exhibit like this that would help your child understand that rainbows are in many places in our world.

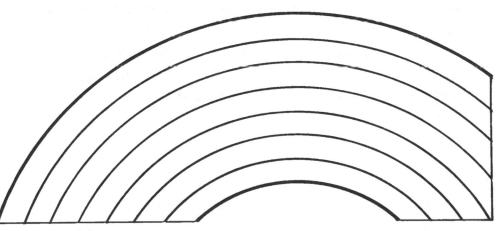

What to Do

Make a Water Rainbow

Why wait until after it rains to see a rainbow? Start up your sprinklers or a fill a squirt bottle with water. Squirt water from a variety of positions until you can see the light reflecting a rainbow.

Make Rainbow Bubbles

You can have your own personal rainbows.

Materials

- ¼ cup Joy® dishwashing liquid
- ¾ cup water
- ½ teaspoon glycerin (available at drugstores)

Directions

Mix the ingredients and let them stand for an hour or two before using. Blow bubbles with plastic straws, berry baskets, slotted spoons, or anything else with a hole in it. As you blow, have your child show you the rainbow in each bubble. If you keep your hands wet, the bubbles will land on them without popping. Quick! What are the colors?

Make Rainbow Shadows

Using colored gels which you can buy at an art supply store, make colored shadows that look like a rainbow on the ground. You can also cut and paste a few gels together, overlapping them for a color-mixing lesson. Once you have shown your child how the paper reflects the color instead of making a black shadow, you won't need to give any more instruction. He'll be off on his own.

What Else?

Your child will enjoy Don Freeman's *A Rainbow of My Own*.

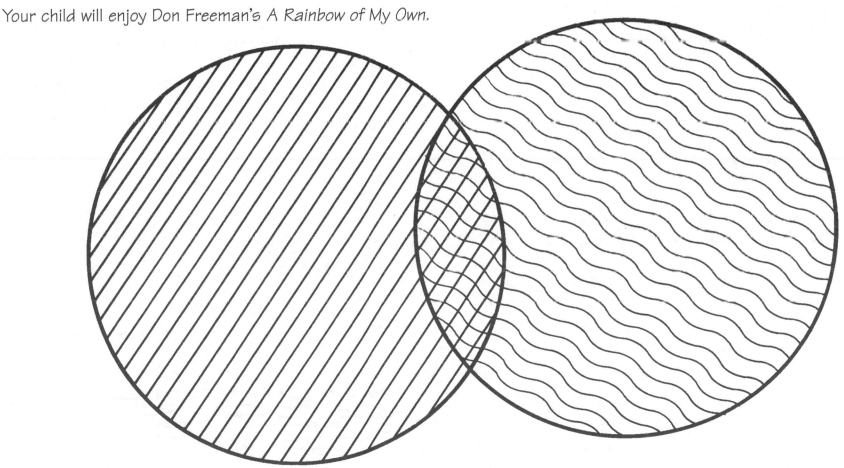

Pretty, Puffy Clouds

We don't usually think much about the purpose of clouds unless they are dumping unwanted water our way. We all know that we wouldn't have rain without the bundles of moisture we call clouds. They are part of the everlasting cycle of water that moves between the earth and the sky.

The next time you see a big, puffy cloud in the sky, ask your child some thought-provoking questions about it: What do you think clouds are made of? What would it feel like to lie on a cloud? Why are clouds white, gray, and multi-colored at sunset? How do clouds make you feel? Although the answers to these questions won't be scientific, they will be great mind-stretchers for your child.

There are numerous categories that meteorologists use to classify clouds and predict fair or foul weather. Three of the major cloud types are *cirrus* (high elevation, wispy, good weather), *cumulus* (puffy, with a flat bottom), and *stratus* (thin, low, moisture-filled, seen on overcast days). Most days you will see a combination of those, as clouds are known for changing with just the slightest blow of the breeze.

Where to Go

The park, field, beach, desert, or any place with a clear view is perfect for cloudgazing. Even a quick ride on the freeway lends itself to cloud games, like naming the shape and watching it change before your very eyes.

Some children's museums have exhibits on evaporation and cloud formations that may be a bit advanced for preschoolers but give a good scientific introduction to the topic. Call around to your local museums to see what they have to offer on this subject.

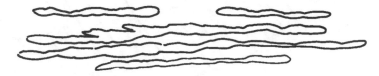

What to Do

Make a Cloud in a Bag

These clouds won't be puffy, but you can demonstrate how real clouds work in your own kitchen.

Materials

- resealable sandwich bag
- freezer
- air

Directions

Open the plastic bag and scoop in some fresh air. Seal the bag tightly. Put it in the freezer for five minutes. Then take it out, open quickly, and blow into it. Quickly seal it again. Look, you've made a cloud!

Make a Cloud Mobile

Hang some cumulus clouds in your child's room.

Materials

- white construction paper
- stapler
- tissue paper or newspaper
- scissors
- coat hanger
- string

Directions

Cut out three pairs of cumulus cloud shapes (puffy on top, flat on bottom). Staple around the tops and sides of the cloud pairs. Stuff the shapes with tissue or newspaper and staple the bottoms closed. Poke a hole in the top of each cloud and attach a piece of string. Tie one end of the string to a coat hanger.

What Else?

Read the children's book classic *It Looked Like Spilt Milk* by Charles G. Shaw, and discover what animals and shapes your child sees.

Let It Snow!

Winter is time for scenes of snow-covered hillsides filled with children sledding on toboggans. The snow is a covering for the earth—a white winter blanket for the slumbering life underneath.

We all know snow is cold, but what exactly is snow and where does it come from? After you have asked your little one these thought-provoking questions you can explain it like this: It has to be very cold to snow—32° F (0° C) or less. When it is 32° F (0° C), the water in the clouds begins to freeze. Crystals of frozen water then join together. When the crystals are heavy enough, they fall gently out of the sky as snowflakes. It is said that no two snowflakes are alike. Your child will find this hard to believe unless you spend time looking at their unique forms under a magnifying glass.

Where to Go

If you don't live in a region where it snows, you will most likely have to go to a higher elevation to find some. Be sure to check road conditions before you travel.

In communities that do not get snow, keep your eyes open for businesses that have promotions by bringing in a snow-making machine. This will provide hours of winter fun where it would not otherwise be experienced. Be sure to bring home a couple of handfuls of the icy mixture for some of the activities described on the following pages.

What to Do

Colored Snowballs

When white gets a little boring, liven up the snow a bit with your child's favorite color.

Materials

- liquid food coloring
- spray bottle

Directions

Fill a spray bottle with water and a few drops of liquid food coloring. Form the snow balls. Turn them to coat with colored water. Alternatively, you could squirt a pattern in the snow with different colors or try mixing colors to get a new effect.

Melting Magic

Even if you don't have snow where you live, you surely have ice cubes. Use them to try this experiment.

Materials

- ice cube
- string
- salt

Directions

Lay pieces of wet string over the ice cube. Sprinkle some salt on it. Count to 30 and lift the string. The ice cube should stick to it. The salt made the ice melt, then it refroze, causing the string to stick.

What Else?

Read the wordless book *The Snowman* by Raymond Briggs.

Melting Snowmen

Bring winter into your warm house and see how long it lasts.

Materials

- washpan filled with snow
- aluminum pie pan
- buttons, raisins, etc., to decorate your mini snowman

Directions

Bring a washpan full of snow into your kitchen. Build a mini snowman in the aluminum pie tin. Use buttons and raisins and whatever else you can think of from your kitchen to create your little snowperson. Make some guesses, then set the timer to see how long it takes for the snowman to melt.

Inspecting Snowflakes

Watch your child's curiosity overflow as you closely look at the facets of a snowflake on a snowy day.

Materials

- black construction paper
- freezer
- magnifying glass

Directions

Freeze the paper and take it outside as a light snow is falling. Hold the paper so that a few snowflakes fall onto it. Bring the paper into the house and look at it under a magnifying glass. Can you see how snowflakes look the same? Different? Can you believe how something so tiny can be so intricate?

What Else?

What is this rhyme talking about?

Roll him and roll him until he is big.

Roll him until he is fat as a pig.

He has two eyes and a hat on his head.

He'll stand there all night while we go to bed.

Make Permanent Snowflakes

These giant snowflakes will glitter and shimmer when you hang them in your window.

Materials

- plastic strawberry basket
- scissors
- white glue
- silver glitter
- thread

Directions

Cut the bottom from the strawberry basket. These can be cut in squares or circles. Smear the basket bottom with glue. Sprinkle glitter on the basket bottom. When the glue dries, repeat glue and glitter on the other side. When complete, hang with a piece of thread.

What Else?

The Snowy Day by Ezra Jack Keats is the story of one boy's magical day in the snow.

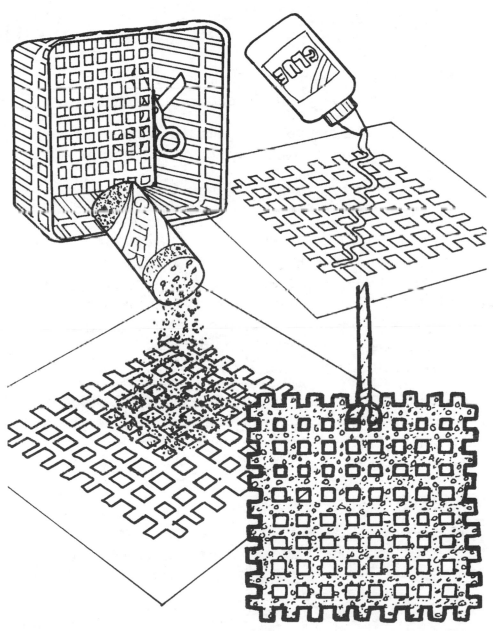

Wind

Wind is constantly changing. It is invisible, yet full of power. It is colorless, yet it fills our world with feeling.

What is wind? You can ask your child this almost impossible question, but you may not get much of an answer. Here is the scientific explanation for the adult: Wind is the movement of air pressure in the atmosphere. Air has weight. Hot air rises upward, and cool air, which is heavier, pushes the hot air even higher. You have probably heard from your local news meteorologist about high-pressure and low-pressure systems. High-pressure usually means clear skies and good weather are ahead. Low pressure is a system where the hot air from high pressure areas mixes with cool and dry air to bring overcast skies, and even rain or snow.

But your child won't care about this. He will just want to know what the wind is and where it comes from. Do your best to explain that wind is the movement of the air pushing on itself.

Where to Go

Have you ever noticed that there is almost always a breeze at the beach? That's because the cool air from above the water is mixing with the warmer air from land, causing movement of the air. Beaches are perfect places for kite flying or other enjoyable wind-friendly activities.

The next time you visit an airport, show your child the wind socks used to show wind direction for the pilots. Wind socks are usually on or near the traffic control tower and the runways. This is a wonderful application of how nature affects people and technology.

What to Do

Make a Pinwheel

Everyone loves to watch the wind work with one of these whimsical toys.

Materials

- 6" x 6" paper square
- brad
- drinking straw
- scissors

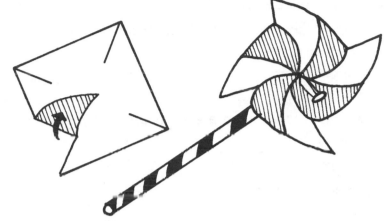

Directions

Number the four corners of the paper, starting with the upper-left and going clockwise. Gently fold the corners together, one to three and two to four. Find the middle of the square and cut halfway up to it from each of the four corners. Fold in every other corner so that they meet in the middle and can be held together with a brad. Poke the brad into a plastic straw. Blow the pinwheel or plant it in your garden to test the wind. (**Note:** Origami paper makes colorful pinwheels.)

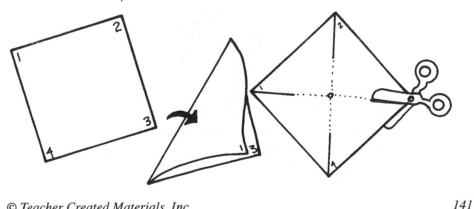

Play a Wind Game

Are you full of hot air? Want to make your own wind? Try this fun game!

Materials

- ping-pong ball
- table

Directions

Sit across from your child, holding your arms out on the table until they meet or almost meet your child's. Keeping your face close to the table, blow the ball back and forth to each other until you are blue in the face and all out of breath.

What Else?

Read *Amy Loves the Wind* by Lillian Hoban. Amy also loves the sun, rain, and snow, as you will see in the other books in the series.

Make a Wind Sock

Test the wind direction with an instrument similar to the one used at airports.

Materials

- clean plastic lid from a sour cream or yogurt container
- scissors
- old nylon stockings
- thin drinking straw
- wide drinking straw
- stapler

Directions

Cut an 8" section from the toe end of one of the stockings. Cut out the center from the container lid, leaving about 1" around the rim. Fit the lid rim inside of the stocking. Staple the wind sock at the covered lid rim to the thin drinking straw. Cut the wide drinking straw so that the wind sock and thin straw poke out through the top when stuck inside the wide straw. Poke the wide straw into the dirt in your garden and insert the thin straw. Watch the wind sock spin with the wind.

Do a Wind Experiment

This demonstration is just the right speed for a preschooler's study of wind.

Materials

- tricycle or other riding toy
- curling ribbon
- scissors

Directions

Choose your child's favorite color of curling ribbon. Cut and curl many, many short lengths. Go outside and tie the ribbons to the handlebars of the child's tricycle. Let your child experiment with the cause and effect of wind on his own machine. (**Note of caution:** It is best to curl many strands of shorter ribbon, rather than a few longer strands. It is vital that none of the strands be long enough to get tangled in the wheels or any other part of the bike.)

Walking with the Stars

Twinkle, twinkle, little star . . . and little planets . . . and little sun and moon. Of course, we know they are not little at all, but we call them little based on what we observe. Isn't it fascinating that the world is so much bigger than just what we see? It is hard to imagine that the planet we live on is a huge, floating ball in space. There are so many stars in the sky that we can't even count them. Concepts like these are too advanced for a preschool mind, but there are many wonderful ways to introduce young children to outer space.

Day or night, the solar system is amazing. Many children speak the word "moon" early on, followed soon after by "sun." The best way for little ones to enjoy the stars, planets, and moon is during a nighttime walk, but the second best—and more up-close—way is through the many wonderful books that have beautiful satellite photographs. The Internet is also an ideal source for at-home explorations (see page 157). Many of the activities in this section of the book will take place at night or in the dark. Young children are usually in bed after dark, but allow them to come out after dark to inspect the nighttime sky. Be sure to have your children warmly clothed, and prepare them for the interesting noises they may hear at night. Above all, stay close, because nothing is scarier than being lost in the dark.

Starry, Starry Night

The sights and sounds of a walk at night are completely different than those heard on the same path by day. It's hard to take a night walk without looking up at the stars. Not only do they make a light that leads you, they also make pretty designs. It's never too early to teach your child about the beauty of the stars.

Astronomy, the study of the stars and planets, is a complicated science, but there are some facts that everyone should know. There are about 3,000 visible stars in the night sky (and 3,000 more visible stars on the other side of the world). Ancient people attempted to understand the universe by analyzing the shapes that the stars seemed to make. These ancient astrologers (as opposed to modern star specialists called astronomers) learned many interesting things about the placement and movement of the nighttime lights. As you watch the stars throughout the year, you will notice, as they did, that the stars are in the same positions every year at the same time. Later in this section you will see some examples of seasonal constellations and be shown how to find them on your own. It will be especially helpful if you learn how to locate the North Star, the brightest star we can see in the night sky.

When you are looking at the stars with your child, ask questions. Some examples include: Where do the stars go during the day? Why don't we see them? Can you find a bear shape among the stars? a dog? a man with a bow and arrow? How big do you think the stars are if you are standing next to them? You will probably find that your child asks you more questions than you ask her.

Where to Go

A mountaintop area that has clear visibility is perfect for stargazing. Be sure to wear warm clothes, even in summer. Take binoculars and, if you can get one, a telescope for an up-close view of the stars and planets. If you can't get to a high elevation, at least leave the city lights to get a good look at the seasonal constellations in the night sky.

Many colleges and universities have some sort of astronomy program set up for the community. See if yours has an observatory where you can see the stars, or if they have lectures for children on stargazing.

What to Do

Make a Flashlight Constellation

Teach your child about the basic constellations with this easy demonstration, and then go outside and see the real thing.

Materials

- flashlight
- pin
- black construction paper

Directions

Cut out a circle 1" larger in diameter than your flashlight. With a pin, poke holes to make the pattern of a simple constellation, like the Big Dipper. Tape the edges all around the outside of the flashlight. Shine the flashlight onto a wall and watch the constellation appear. Can you find the same one outside?

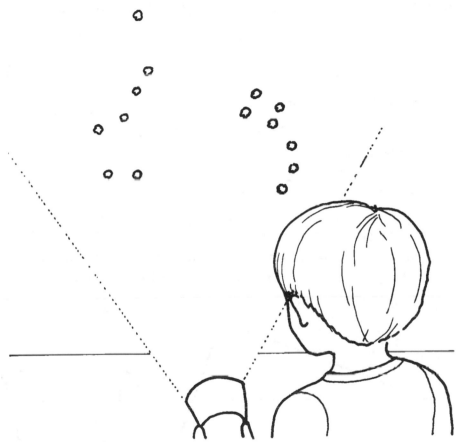

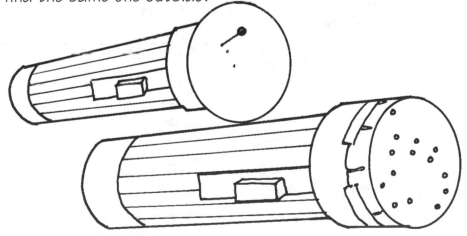

What Else?

Can you count the stars? How far can you get? There are over 3,000 stars visible in the night sky, so your child shouldn't get discouraged if he or she loses track.

Create Your Own Constellation

Once youngsters understand the idea of identifying pictures in the stars, they will want to create their own.

Materials

- dark blue or black construction paper
- small gold or silver star stickers
- white pencil.

Directions

Give your child some star stickers, and give him a piece of construction paper which he will use to symbolize the sky. Tell him to imagine a picture on the paper and to place stars to show important points. Then he can connect the stars with a white pencil.

Do a Demonstration of Light

Why can't you see the stars during the day? Do this activity to demonstrate. On a bright day, go outside and shine a flashlight. Can you see the light? Then go into the house and find a dark room or closet. Shine the flashlight there. What a difference! Ask your child to explain why you could see the light inside but not outside. Stars are in the sky all of the time, but the sun shines so brightly, it drowns out the light from the stars.

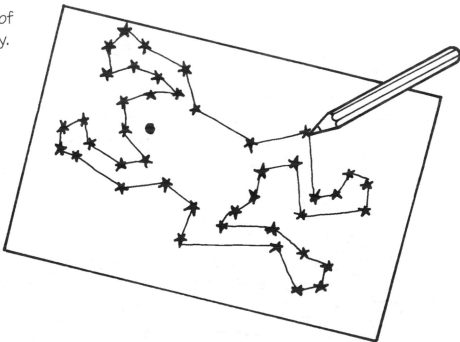

What Else?

Read Iza Trapani's *Twinkle, Twinkle Little Star*.

Find Some Constellations

A night looking at the stars wouldn't be complete without finding and labeling at least one constellation. Here's a simple guide to a couple of the most popular and easiest-to-locate constellations.

What Else?

A good book about constellations for families is *Glow-in-the-Dark Constellations* by C. E. Thompson. Also available is Clint Hatchetts' *The Glow-in-the-Dark Night Sky Book*. In both books, the constellations shine when you go outside at night. Constellations are arranged seasonally, so it will be easy to find them.

The Big Dipper

The Little Dipper

The Northern Cross

The Man in the Moon

The Earth's moon has been a source of folklore and mystery for centuries. It will take many decades of research, to uncover many mysteries of the moon. But now that people have been there and back, there are some wonderful things about the moon that we know and can share with young children.

Someday your child might actually visit the moon. When she gets there, what will she find? A place with no water, no air, and very little gravity to keep things from floating away. It is not the big, lit-up ball that it appears to be from Earth. The moon has a sandy, bumpy surface, with many rocky mountains and deep craters.

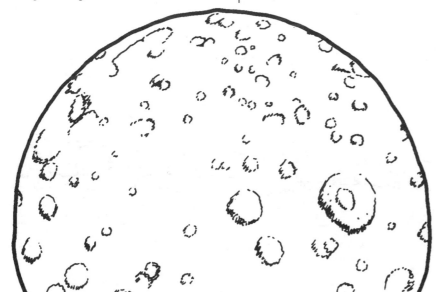

For centuries, people have conjectured about how the moon received its interesting contours. Your child will have fun trying to guess about how they happened, as well. There are stories about the texture and taste of the moon. What does your little one think the moon would taste like? How long would it take to get there? What would she see when she does get there? How would she travel once she had launched? Moon stories are fun to develop and share.

Where to Go

As with stargazing, any area with high elevation, clear visibility, and distance from city lights will be a good place to look at the moon closely. Hopefully, there is somewhere near where you live where you can look at the moonrise most nights. It is magical to watch the moonrise from your own yard, if you have that option.

Since you can't go to the moon (yet!), try some Internet sites listed in the resource section of this book. These will help you as you explain the moon's surface and texture to your child.

What to Do

Make Moon Craters

It is speculated that the moon's craters, some of which are miles across, were made by meteorites. You can get the effect on a very small scale with this activity.

Materials

- plaster of Paris
- sturdy cardboard box
- marbles and small rocks

Directions

Mix the plaster according to the directions on the package. Pour plaster into the box, covering the bottom completely. Drop the marbles and rocks into the plaster from different heights. Lift the marbles out gently. When the plaster is completely dry, your child can run his cars and trucks over the surface of his own moon.

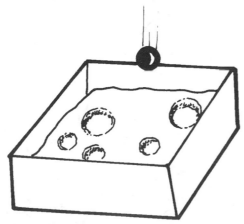

Show the Moon's Phases

Watch the moon change nightly right before your very eyes.

Materials

- bar of soap
- window facing the moon

Directions

Start this activity at the full moon stage. Set a time each night or every couple of nights (for example, right before your child's bedtime) to go to the window and look at the moon. Talk about its brightness and what it looks like: a ball, a fingernail paring, an orange section, etc. Then take a bar of soap and make a circle of the same size each night. Color in the part of the moon that is lit. Like magic, you will watch the shape reduce over time. When you are done with your moon pictures, the soap will wash off easily with a little elbow grease.

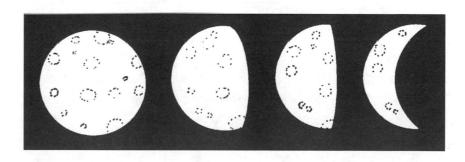

Demonstrate How the Moon Gives Light

Your child will have a hard time understanding that the moon does not have its own light, but this demonstration will help. You will need three people to complete this activity.

Materials

- globe
- hand mirror
- flashlight

Direction

Each person will hold one of the three items. The globe represents the Earth, the flashlight is the sun, and the mirror is the moon. Stand in a triangle formation. Point the flashlight at the mirror. Since it is nighttime, the sun will not shine on the Earth but will be reflected by the moon, just as the flashlight is reflected in the mirror. For an extra challenge, see if you can get the moon to shine on your state or country.

What Else?

Ancient peoples have seen many things in the moon, such as a face, a bear, and a woman holding her child. When you look at the moon, what do you see?

Make a Flip Book of the Moon

Copy this page and cut out the squares. Stack them in order, and then staple them in the upper left corner. Show your child how to flip through from back to front to watch the moon phases change.

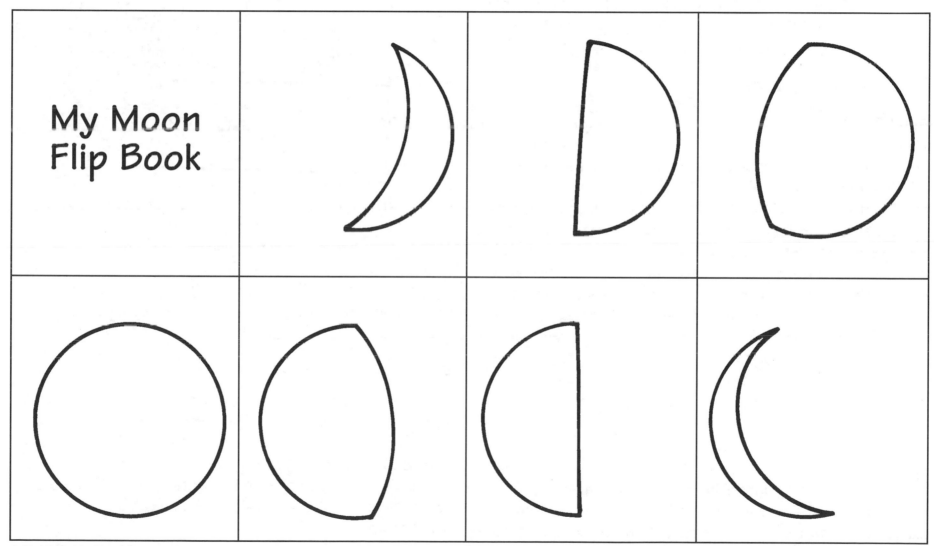

Extensions of Nature

Now that you have developed a love of nature in yourself and your preschooler, you will want to build on his curiosity and knowledge in a tangible and permanent way. Below you will find some ways to collect and keep nature with you for as long as you like.

Nature Collections

Egg Cartons

These are convenient houses for many of your small collectibles. The benefits are that items are easily moved around and changed, a must for small children. Perfect for this type of collection container are shells, rocks, bark pieces, seeds, and pods. You can mix all types of items in a single egg carton or, if your child is a true collector, you can encourage having a separate carton for each type of collectible. If your nature lover is also a budding artist, encourage him to decorate the carton in any way that will make it more special. You can paint the entire container (cardboard egg cartons work better than polystyrene) or cover it with stickers. Best of all, egg cartons are recycled, free, and a small investment for the new collector.

Milk Cartons

A perfect option for larger items is a milk carton collector box. Choose a reasonable number of sections, like six or nine. You must use clean cardboard boxes that

are all the same size. Cut the top off of each carton. An adult can hot glue the cartons together to make cubbies. This type of collection box is perfect for a number of items you want to put together (like feathers) as well as single larger items (like old, abandoned bird nests). Once you dry your favorite flowers, one of the cubbies would make a nice place to keep them.

Plastic Boxes

This type of container is perfect for larger items that you want to keep indefinitely. If you want to protect special items from nature, like seashells, crystals, or abandoned bird nests, it is best to wrap them in tissue paper or bubble wrap and place them in plastic boxes. These are not optimal for display purposes but are fine for long-term storage.

Journal Writing Activities

When you think of journal, perhaps you think of an unillustrated book with pages and pages of adult thoughts. A preschool journal is different; it is valuable because it will probably be the first book that he makes by himself. This special book will be filled with pictures, photographs, ideas, and dictated adventures. It can be decorated with pens, crayons, and stickers. Copy page 154 to get started.

Drawings of his favorite animals, season, or place to walk would be great journal additions. Feel free to add your own pages that are inspired by your little one's experiences in nature.

There are a number of ways to bind the final journal. You can staple it across the sides or top. You can also use a three-hole punch and binder rings, which will allow you to keep adding pages. If you would like to preserve this journal, laminate the pages with clear shelf paper or take it to a store that provides this service.

If you are especially proud of your little one's accomplishment, make duplicate books by color-copying the pages. This will be a huge hit with grandparents. Even if you don't make copies, be sure your child shares his printed work with anyone who will listen. Making a book with your child is simple, fun, and a wonderful memory maker.

Preserving Your Nature Time Together

While you are on your nature walks, you have been experiencing many things together. Hopefully, you have been able to catch many of those things on film. Have two copies made of photos and put one set into mini albums that your child can keep.

If you have a cassette player that is small enough, bring it along on your walks to capture sounds in nature. You can play them back later to see if your child can identify them.

Make a video of a nature process, like hatching caterpillars or charting the moon's stages. Many of the activities in this book take place over days or weeks and lend themselves naturally to homemade nature videos.

My Nature Journal

Name_____

What Can I Do?

We have learned that the Earth is a big and beautiful place. During your walks and other experiences in nature, you have seen how things change and how things rely on each other to just stay alive on our Earth. But as you have walked along, you have probably noticed that some things are harmful to nature. Have you seen something as simple as trash discarded on the ground at the side of a road? Have you noticed oil or pollution in a lake or stream? Have you seen how housing tracts go farther and deeper inside hillside canyons, crowding out the wildlife that has called that area home?

How can you help your child feel a responsibility for the Earth and all of the wonderful elements of nature you experience together? Here are some helpful hints and activities.

What to Do

First, you must set an example as someone who takes care of things in nature. Parents are the role models to their young children. We must model respect and care for the Earth by taking care of trash (i.e., recycling glass, plastic, and aluminum.) You can also report animal neglect and emergencies, like sea gulls injured on a beach. These are some simple ways to show your child that you care about the world.

Here are a couple of fun activities to show your child how to take better care of the world in which we live.

Sort Plastic Containers

Did you know that most plastic is recyclable? Look on the bottom of the package or lid for the recycle symbol. Inside of the symbol is a number. Have your child sort the various containers into piles by that number. This is what happens to the containers once they get to the recycling plant. For your child, it will also be good sorting practice.

Visit a Dump or Landfill

It sounds disgusting, but it isn't! Dumps are fascinating to children because junk intrigues them. You will need permission to look around, but once you do, your child will have a million "What is that?" questions. And landfills, contrary to popular belief, do not stink! The refuse is covered each day to keep out insects and birds, so the scent is very minimal. Both of these places would be fabulous field trips for your child. Remember to look, but not touch!

Copy and add this page to your child's nature journal.

This is what I can do to protect the Earth.

References and Resources

Magazines

Chickadee. The Young Naturalist Foundation c/o Owl Chickadee Magazines, 255 Great Arrow Avenue, Buffalo, NY 14027.

Family Fun. P.O. Box 37032, Boone, IA 50037–0032.

National Geographic World. National Geographic Society. 17th & M Streets NW, Washington, D.C. 20036.

Web Sites

The National Zoo at www.si.edu/natzoo (a Smithsonian site with photographs of animals and their habitats)

StarChild at http://starchild.gsfc.nasa.gov/docs/StarChild/StarChild.html (not intended for preschoolers, but the photos are spectacular; good introduction to the Internet for children)

National Park Service at http://www.nps.gov/

Redwood National and State Parks at http://www.nps.gov/redw/

Yellowstone National Part at http://www.nps.gov/yell/index.htm

Photos of endangered and threatened species at http://www.fwp.mt.gov/kids/kids.htm

Resources

Ardley, Neil. *The Science Book of Water.* Harcourt Brace Jovanovich, 1991.

Bourgeois, Paulette. *The Moon.* Kids Can Press, 1997.

Drake, Jane & Ann Love. *The Kids' Summer Handbook.* Ticknore & Fields, 1994.

Lovejoy, Sharon. *Sunflower Houses: Garden Discoveries for Children of All Ages.* Interweave Press, 1991.

Shedd, Warner. *The Kids' Wildlife Book.* Williamson Publishing, 1994.

Thompson, C.E. *Glow-in-the-Dark Constellations.* Grosset & Dunlap, 1989.

Wyler, Rose. *Puddles and Ponds.* Simon and Schuster, 1990.

Young, Ruth. *Hands-On Minds-On Science: Rocks and Minerals.* Teacher Created Materials, 1994.

Young, Ruth. *Science Is Fun.* Teacher Created Materials, 1999. (That's what the book says)

Nature Sources and Catalogs

Carolina Biological Supply Company
(800) 334-5551
2700 York Road
Burlington, NC 27215-3398 or
P.O. Box 187
Gladstone, OR 97027-0187

Hearth Song
(800)325-2502
6519 N. Galena Rd., P.O. Box 1773
Peoria, IL 61656-1773
(ask for catalog; nature supplies and games and activities for all children of all ages)

Insect Lore
(800)LIVE BUG
P.O. Box 1535
Shafter, CA 93263
http://www.insectlore.com
(supplies butterfly larva, ant farms, tadpoles, silkworm eggs, and many other wonderful materials to use in nature activities)

National Wildlife Federation
1400 26th St. NW
Washington, D.C. 20036 2266
(Write for information on any variety of nature topics.)

Shepherd's Garden Seeds
(408)335-6910
6116 Highway 9
Felton, CA 95018
(send $1.00 for catalog; specializes in children gardens)

Bibliography

Many of these books are listed in the text, and all of them have been specially chosen to read with preschoolers. You will find something for every area of nature study.

Barrett, Judi. *Cloudy with a Chance of Meatballs.* Aladdin Books, 1978.

Bourgeoise, Paulette. *The Moon.* Kids Can Press Ltd., 1997.

Briggs, Raymond. *The Snowman.* Random House, 1978.

Cannon, Janell. *Stellaluna.* Harcourt Brace, 1993.

Carle, Eric. *Eric Carle's Animals, Animals.* Philomel Books, 1998.

Carle, Eric. *The Very Hungry Caterpillar.* Philomel Books, 1969. (**Note:** All Eric Carle books are wonderful choices to read to preschoolers; most of them have animals or nature as their topics.)

Carlstrom, Nancy White. *What Would You Do If You Lived at the Zoo?* Little, Brown & Co., 1994.

Caseley, Judith. *Grandpa's Garden Lunch.* Greenwillow Books, 1990.

Delaney, A. *Pearl's First Prize Plant.* HarperCollins, 1997.

Ehlert, Lois. *Eating the Alphabet.* Harcourt Brace & Co., 1989.

Ehlert, Lois. *Planting a Rainbow.* Harcourt Brace Jovanovish, 1988.

Ehlert, Lois. *Red Leaf, Yellow Leaf.* Harcourt Brace & Co., 1991. (**Note:** Lois Ehlert has written several beautiful, bold nature books for children. Any of her titles would be appropriate for preschoolers.)

Freeman, Don. *A Rainbow of My Own.* Viking Press, 1966.

Gachenbach, Dick. *Mighty Tree.* Harcourt Brace Jovanovich, 1992.

Gans, Roma. *Rock Collecting.* Thomas Y. Crowell, 1984.

Guarino, Deborah. *Is Your Mama a Llama?* Scholastic, 1989.

Hatchett, Clint. *The Glow-in-the-Dark Night Sky Book.* Random House, 1988.

Hendrich, Mary Jean. *If Anything Ever Goes Wrong at the Zoo.* Harcourt Brace & Co., 1993.

Hoban, Julia. *Amy Loves the Wind.* 1989.

Hoberman, Mary Ann. *A House Is a House for Me.* Puffin Books, 1982.

James, Simon. *Dear Mr. Blueberry.* Aladdin, 1991.

James, Simon. *The Wild Woods.* Candlewich Press, 1993.

Kalan, Robert. *Rain.* Greenwillow Books, 1978.

Keats, Ezra Jack. *Pet Show.* Aladdin, 1972.